P9-CCI-313

NEVER EASY, NEVER PRETTY

NEVER EASY, NEVER PRETTY

A FAN, A CITY, A CHAMPIONSHIP SEASON

Dean Bartoli Smith

With a Foreword by Stan Charles

TEMPLE UNIVERSITY PRESS
PHILADELPHIA

TEMPLE UNIVERSITY PRESS
Philadelphia, Pennsylvania 19122
www.temple.edu/tempress

Published 2013

ISBN 978-1-4399-1106-8 (hardcover)
ISBN 978-1-4399-1108-2 (e-book)

Cataloging-in-Publication Data available from the Library of Congress

∞ The paper used in this publication meets the requirements of the American National Standard for Information Sciences—Permanence of Paper for Printed Library Materials, ANSI Z39.48-1992

Printed in the United States of America

2 4 6 8 9 7 5 3 1

For Christina, Mary Julia, and Quinn

Contents

Foreword

Stan Charles

LET'S BE perfectly blunt: writing a book about a Baltimore professional sports team winning a championship isn't an easy endeavor. The 2012 Ravens season was never thought of as some sort of slam-dunk time for the franchise to jump up and win its second Super Bowl. In fact, Baltimore fans and the sports media generally believed that the 2010 and 2011 Ravens teams were much closer to winning a championship than the team that took the field in September 2012. Recently published coffee-table books on the subject contain hastily collected assemblages of photos and articles, but to put together everything that happened to the 2012 Ravens—from the death of the franchise's original owner, Art Modell, to the retirement of linebacker Ray Lewis—you need a keen and discerning eye.

Dean Bartoli Smith is to be applauded for all that *Never Easy, Never Pretty: A Fan, A City, A Championship Season* captures about the Ravens' Super Bowl run in 2012.

In these pages Smith gives us the thinking fan's perspective on the players, the games, and the city as the season progressed. Most importantly, he shows why our teams are so darned important to us and how they inspire us to drudge through lives that pale in comparison with these moments that are so, so special.

There are special moments in this book that will stick with me like adhesive tape on skin. Smith writes with passion about the relationship between Ray Lewis and Ray Rice within the context of the running back making an impossible first down on fourth and 29 against the Chargers. He chronicles the rise of receiver and kick returner Jacoby Jones, from his release by the Texans to his status as a superstar in Baltimore. He tells the story of Ray's "Last Dance" with intensity and emotion. He dares to broach the subject of the similarities between Johnny Unitas and Joe Flacco with members of the Colts 1958 Championship team and takes us inside the Superdome in New Orleans for one of the greatest Super Bowls in NFL history.

We always hear how nothing brings a community together more than its tribal sports franchise's pursuit of a championship. Sports, by its very nature, gives each town participating some sort of "hope springs eternal" feeling at the beginning of every season. The Ravens are a relatively young franchise, with only 17 seasons under their belt, and the team has been embraced by younger generations of fans. Smith goes outside the stadium and provides insight into the depth of the city's relationship to its football team and how that team has all but erased the pain of the Colts' leaving in 1984.

That is Dean's story to tell. He comes from a long line of Baltimore football fans who began following the Colts in the early 1950s. He is the son of a former college basketball coach, and while that might not seem relevant, Dean and his father have spent much of their time together on this earth analyzing the machinations of Baltimore sports teams, including the Colts and the Ravens. He is also a distinguished man of letters, with a degree in English literature from the University of Virginia and a master's in poetry from Columbia University.

Though Dean may have the sensibility of a poet, his real skill in this book is not in telling the exact story as it happened; it's more like the work of a great musical conductor. Along the way, he presents a unique collection of ex-Colts, ex-Ravens, Baltimore sports media, and fans. He shares interviews with Ravens Roost members who put the same life and breath into their Roosts as did those old Colts Corral fan clubs that started this thing more than 60 years ago. He also blends in the voices of current Ravens players and coaches—Joe Flacco, Ray Lewis, Ray Rice, Terrell Suggs, and John Harbaugh—as the season progresses to its exhilarating conclusion.

So, by using not just his words but the words of others, Dean is able not only to tell the story of how this past season evolved into such a monumental happening but also to offer many points of view about how it all unfolded.

Never Easy, Never Pretty takes us on Smith's personal football odyssey, one that spans four decades, from the North Baltimore practice fields of the Baltimore Colts in 1970 to the banks of the Mississippi and the Ravens' second Super Bowl win in 2013. It's a love letter to the city from a guy whose Baltimore football roots go deep.

NEVER EASY, NEVER PRETTY

Introduction

The groom looks confident
like Johnny Unitas among the masses
gathered quickly to witness
another miraculous comeback . . .
underneath the roses in your gloved hands
my unexpected feet kick.

—Dean Bartoli Smith

AT 4 A.M. on Sunday, February 3, 2013, I got out of bed and checked the impact of the overnight snow showers. I hadn't slept much, worried about the San Francisco 49ers offense with a mobile Colin Kaepernick at quarterback and a diverse array of weaponry that would challenge an aging Ravens defense in Super Bowl XLVII. A thin sheet of snow was scattered across Charles Street.

I showered and put on my clean number 82 Torrey Smith jersey. Choosing a Ravens jersey had been challenging. I had spent months trying to decide which player would last the longest in the salary-cap driven NFL and settled on a wide receiver with my last name. The two-week hiatus between the AFC Championship and the Super Bowl had forced me to wash it, which went against my superstitious nature.

Now I was flying to New Orleans to see the game in person. The game tickets and flight cost me $2,000, but my lodging in the suburb of Metairie was going to be free, courtesy of a college friend who loves the Saints. I had scoured every ticket site for days and waited until the last minute, when tickets in the 200 level behind the end zone dropped by $500 on the Thursday before the game.

My six-year-old son had asked several times to go, and I felt guilty for not taking him with me. We had watched the Ravens games together, but this trip was an extravagant expense amid a litany of bills for private tuition, camps, and activities. I kissed my sleeping wife and children goodbye and headed toward the airport.

At 4:30 A.M. the abandoned streets of Baltimore glistened with moisture. A little more than a month before, the Ravens had been mired in a losing streak and were not a part of any sports talk show discussions evaluating the best teams in the NFL. The last thing on my mind at that point was a trip to the Super Bowl. Then the Ravens fired their offensive coordinator, announced the retirement of the franchise's greatest player, and made one of the more dramatic runs in NFL history.

As I moved into the left lane for the BWI airport exit, a car full of late-night revelers pulled up next to me, honking their horns, yelling out the window "Go Ravens!" and waving—one final connection to a city that had "gone Raven" and had lost its mind for football. They had seen my trunk magnet and they knew where I was headed.

Once inside the airport, I saw purple jerseys appearing in the corridors: Flaccos, Rices, Ngatas, and Lewises. I felt at home and lucky to be headed for the first time in my life to one of the greatest sporting events in the world. I thought of the Colts fans in my family who loved football and how they had inspired me to make the journey.

My love affair with Baltimore football began at age 7 in the summer of 1970, when my father took me to see the Baltimore Colts practice one afternoon. After breaking training camp at Western Maryland College, they were preparing for the season at the University of Baltimore's athletic fields off Rogers Avenue, in a neighborhood called Mount Washington.

Before that late summer practice, I knew that the New York Jets had shocked the Colts 16–7 in Super Bowl III more than a year before. The game still perplexed the ladies under the beehive dryers in my Italian grandmother's basement beauty salon and was fresh on the tongues of my Irish father's cronies at the Belvedere Tavern. I listened at the bar over a Shirley Temple.

"Morrall had Jimmy Orr wide open in the end zone," said my father's friend Doc Pyle, who carried a pistol in his medical kit.

"I don't know how he missed him," said my father. "I heard they had some late nights in Miami Beach."

My dad had left his sales job at Esso a few weeks before the 1970 Colts had arrived back in town, choosing to follow his passion and become an assistant coach with the University of Baltimore Bees basketball team. He had also recently separated from my mother, whom he had met in Ocean City, Maryland, just seven years before. She had driven her friends to the seaside resort in a royal blue Thunderbird—her prize possession in the summer of 1962. My father had charmed her with his buzz cut and horn-rims. He made her laugh.

Before they met, my mother had dreams of becoming a lawyer. Soon enough she learned that a baby was in her near future—me. This discovery put her law career on hold indefinitely and meant selling her beloved car.

On the day after I was born—September 22, 1963—the Colts beat the 49ers 20–14 in Golden Gate Park's Kezar Stadium. Quarterback Johnny Unitas engineered a 10-point fourth-quarter comeback to give Don Shula his first win as the youngest head coach in the NFL.

My dad had begun following the Colts when the NFL's Dallas Texans moved to Baltimore in 1953. The original Baltimore Colts had played in the All-America Football Conference from 1947 to 1950 but were disbanded by the league. The '53 franchise resurrected the Colts nickname that been selected in 1947 in a contest that drew 1,887 suggestions. My father's aunt, the late Carita Smith, bought season tickets in 1953, and my dad barely missed a game until 1970. The only exceptions were two "visiting Sundays" at the convent at Mount Saint Agnes College to see his older sister Patricia, a Sister of Mercy.

Aunt Carita worked for the Bendix Corporation making radios, and she carried a flask of peppermint schnapps to the games. She was the sort of fan who in 1960 ripped her brother-in-law Tom Fox's shirt as they watched Green Bay Packer quarterback Lamar McHan run for a 35-yard touchdown against the Colts on a black-and-white TV.

My Aunt Pat, or Sister MacAuley as she was called, remembers Carita's visits to the convent. "Carita was a fanatical Colts fan. When I entered the convent in 1956, we could have visitors only once a month. It was always very 'decorous' except when Carita was there and there was a Colts game. She had a small transistor radio. I remember her jumping up and screaming either in joy or despair. Not your typical convent parlor scene."

My father almost missed a game against the Los Angeles Rams in 1968 because Carita had given her extra ticket to Tom Fox, perhaps still making amends for the torn shirt. It was a big game—the Rams were undefeated—and tickets were scarce. My father remembers fans climbing on top of the generators and scaling the fencing to watch from the mezzanine level outside the stadium.

He and his friend Dorsey Baldwin snuck into the game. Dorsey's uncle, a captain in the Baltimore police department, told the boys to meet him at the handicapped entrance. My father threw a blanket over his friend and wheeled him in. Once inside, they waited for the introductions and then ditched the wheelchair, climbing to the top of the stadium to stand in the aisles and watch the game. The Colts won 27–10 en route to a 13–1 season and that fateful trip to the Super Bowl against Joe Namath and the Jets.

In the summer of 1970 I was just a kid entering second grade and was enduring my own streak of bad luck. Joe Namath had beaten the Colts in January 1969. The Baltimore Orioles lost to

Tom Seaver and the Mets in the 1969 World Series. The Bullets lost to the Knicks in the playoffs the following spring. And before I went to see the Colts that summer, my parents had gone their separate ways and the Beatles, my favorite band, had broken up.

My dad drove me to the Colts' preseason practice in his navy blue Chevy Malibu with a crushed back bumper from when he'd backed it into a telephone pole one night. We parked on a hill overlooking the field where you could see all the Colts going through drills. After practice I waited until the players came off the field and asked for their autographs. I got most of the team and all my favorites: Bubba Smith, John Mackey, Ray May, Billy Ray Smith, Rick Volk, Jerry Logan, Tom Matte, Earl Morrall, and Johnny Unitas.

On that day Unitas was the last one to finish. I could see him across the practice field, working with linebacker Mike Curtis, who carried him on his back up a hill that was stepped with wooden planks to serve as bleachers. Unitas then put Curtis on his back and lumbered up the bleacher steps. They finally finished and headed toward me. The sweat had soaked through Mike Curtis's gray T-shirt. Unitas had on a white shirt.

"Does he want to carry my equipment?" Johnny Unitas asked my dad. I was barely able to move, but somehow I carried his helmet and shoulder pads back to the locker room.

The 1970 season turned out to be a Super Bowl year. My father, my brother, and I watched the Colts play the Dallas Cowboys for the championship at my Uncle Buddy's house out in the country off Jarrettsville Pike. Down 6–0, Unitas threw a pass over receiver Eddie Hinton's head. Hinton tipped the ball toward Cowboy cornerback Mel Renfro, who tapped the ball into tight end John Mackey's hands for a 65-yard touchdown.

The Colts tied the score late in the fourth quarter after a Rick Volk interception took the ball to the Cowboys' 2-yard line and fullback Tom Nowatzke went in. Rookie Jim O'Brien kicked the winning field goal in a sloppily played game that featured 11 turnovers. "It was the ugliest Super Bowl ever," said former Colts announcer Vince Bagli. "O'Brien wasn't a famous kicker at all. He made a couple of kicks. There were fumbles and tipped passes."

Former Giants, Eagles, and Rams punter Sean Landeta remembered the kids in his Baltimore neighborhood all wanting to become field goal kickers after O'Brien's heroics. "We kicked them through goalposts, over volleyball nets, over clotheslines—anywhere we could after O'Brien won the game. We all wanted to be him." We were spoiled back then—the Colts, Orioles, and Bullets all had championship caliber teams. We thought it would never end.

In the summer of 1971 my dad left Baltimore to coach basketball with Paul Baker at Wheeling College in West Virginia. He took me out back at my grandmother's house in Northwood, and we played catch with his football—"The Duke." He told me he was leaving to pursue his coaching dream. "There's a kid in my class whose father moved away," I said. "He doesn't see him very much."

"I wish I could take you with me. This is my dream, son. I need to pursue it. Someday you'll understand."

With Dad gone, I started playing catch with my Aunt Carol, his younger sister, a Sister of Mercy like my Aunt Pat. I had two aunts who were nuns and a father who was a sports fanatic. Aunt Carol was also a tomboy. She threw long bombs to me on Saturday afternoons at the Mercy convalescent home off of Bellona Avenue. She taught me how to run square outs and post patterns. She bought me the greatest present of my youth, a pair of Rawlings shoulder pads. I would come home from school and put on my football uniform with full pads, including the number 19 John Unitas jersey from Hutzler's department store.

During pick-up games our neighbor Mr. Seible played on my team. I had a pretty bad temper in the days after my father left and called Mr. Seible a "bastard" just because I didn't catch a pass he threw to me. I was getting ready to begin third grade and we lived in Courthouse Square Apartments in Towson.

Chuck Seible had been a marine in Vietnam, and he kept the head of a rattlesnake in a jar on his dresser. After my outburst he walked off the field and went home. But before he left he told me to tell my mother what had happened and then come to his house after dinner and apologize to him. If I didn't, he would tell her himself. I can still see the doorbell of the apartment; it took me several minutes to drum up the courage to ring it. I sat down in an empty chair next to his as he was finishing dinner. Mrs. Seible was in the kitchen, and little baby Amy was in her high chair. A white tablecloth covered the table.

"I'm sorry, Mr. Seible, . . . for what I said."

"You need to help out your mom and your brother. You can't be getting angry and saying bad words over a pick-up football game." I understood what he was saying, but during that time, with my father gone, winning and losing meant everything to me. When the Colts lost, it reinforced his absence; when I lost I just got mad.

My brother Brendan and I played football everywhere—on tennis courts, in parking lots, on a grass plot that bordered an alley in Northwood where my grandmother lived. I chipped my four upper teeth when Tolly Nicklas tackled me on a field next to a golf course we played on. If there was no one to play a full game with, my brother and I played one-on-one football.

For most of the fall season in Baltimore, football was on our minds all the time. If we weren't playing or watching a game, we played table football with a matchbook. I sketched Colts helmets, players, and football fields with goalposts in my notebooks and on book covers. During class I would scribble all over the "field" and draw lines through the intersecting points that wove their way toward the end zone as the teacher lectured. Football was ingrained in my imagination.

My brother and I spent weekends with my father's mother. Queenie Smith watched football with us while we ate her signature Irish spaghetti—pasta with meat sauce. "That Johnny Unitas led more comebacks than Carters has liver pills," she would say.

It was at my grandmother's that I became mesmerized by *The NFL Game of the Week*, which featured John Facenda's famous "voice of God" and the slow-motion depiction of the game itself. I remember one sequence when the camera focused on a Terry Bradshaw pass and the slow spin of the ball in solitary flight toward its target—a game both brutal and elegant in the same moment.

We also watched football games with our Italian grandparents on my mother's side of the family, Dino and Carolyn Bartoli. Carolyn, or "Nana" as we used to call her, would get so nervous listening to Johnny Unitas lead a late-game comeback that she would hide under the beehive dryers in her basement beauty shop screaming, "Oh Dino, I can't stand it anymore. The suspense is too much. I can't bear it." Or she would go to her bedroom and pray the rosary until the game was over.

They loved Gino Marchetti and Alan Ameche and always talked about them. They were so proud that Italian Americans were good at football, and my grandmother loved watching Marchetti make a tackle. "I loved those rugged old guys," Nana would tell me decades later, with her mind beginning to fail, "Marchetti, Ameche, and Unitas."

On most Sundays when the Colts were in town she also prepared her legendary crab cakes and homemade gnocchi with "gravy" (spaghetti sauce) for her brother Bernard Ciampi and her cousin Leonard Cerullo, who would drive down from Berwick, Pennsylvania, to watch the Colts games.

Stories about "Cousin Lenny" permeated my childhood. My mother swore that he could walk onto the field at Memorial Stadium untouched and sit on the Colts bench next to the players. "No one ever figured out how he got there, and he never told anyone where he was going," my mother said. He sometimes traveled with bodyguards who wore overcoats and fedoras. He owned a company that made ribbon and fabric, and he provided our family with a lifetime supply of both.

Soon after their separation, my mother and father started dating other people. One day Mom informed my brother and me that we would be going out to dinner with a Baltimore Colt named John Andrews. I'm not sure when or how she met him; at the time she was earning her degree at Morgan State College and working at Ordell Braase's Flaming Pit as a waitress.

Braase had played defensive end for the Colts until 1968, and "The Pit" was often filled with current and former players. Besides that, many of the players lived among us. They shopped at the same grocery stores and their children played against us on sports teams. As a kid I must have met backup quarterback Earl Morrall five times.

John Andrews played running back and tight end for the Colts. My brother and I were very excited. On their first and only date with Brendan and me along, Andrews took us to Johnny Unitas's Golden Arm restaurant. It was a great place to go as a kid because all the helmets from the NFL were displayed on the walls and players like Bubba Smith and John Mackey often came there. And the restaurant served something for dessert called a "snowball" that included coconut shavings and warm chocolate syrup over vanilla ice cream.

This was the first time my brother and I had ever had dinner with an African American person. My mother looked like Cher, beautiful with her long and wild Italian black hair. Andrews wore a metallic grayish blue shirt that was open at the collar. My mother remembers that the dining room hushed when we walked in. She felt that all eyes were on her. This was Baltimore four years removed from the race riots of 1968.

The waitress became flustered at one point and dropped a stack of plates next to our table. Johnny Unitas stopped by and autographed pictures for my brother and me. He looked relaxed and enjoyed talking to people in the restaurant.

Johnny liked John Andrews and patted him on the shoulder. The night was going very well until my brother decided to tell a joke. He was only 6 years old and I knew what was coming. He had only one or two jokes in his entire canon. I kicked him under the table and tried to stop him several times, but my mother intervened. "Your brother is allowed to tell a joke," she said. "Now be quiet."

"Mom, you're going to be sorry," I tried to tell her.

"Dean, let your brother have his time with Mr. Andrews."

"What did Abraham Lincoln say when he saw the first black man?" He looked at John Andrews for approval.

"What did he say, Brendan?" My mother asked with a worried look.

"Bless my heart, bless my soul, I see a . . ."

"That's enough!" hushed my mother, finally grasping the situation. She put her hand around my brother's mouth before he could finish the punch line and led him into the ladies' room for a discussion. This was her worst nightmare.

"Sorry about that," I said to Mr. Andrews. The joke had made its way to the bus stops and halls of Padonia Elementary, where we both went to school.

This was my first encounter with racism. The fact that John Andrews and Johnny Unitas had different colors of skin made no difference on Sundays at Memorial Stadium. Only the touchdowns and the field goals mattered. But a white woman dining with a black man—no matter who they were—was still taboo in Baltimore.

"It's okay," he said and smiled. The night had been ruined. I had visions of going to a Colts game, of playing catch with John Andrews. I just wanted to talk football with someone. But that was the last time my brother and I saw him. My mother dated him a few more times without us.

"He wanted to be a part of our lives," she said, "He was crazy about you and your brother and he was a very nice man. But I had just met Larry." Mom met Larry, her husband to this day, at the Tom Jones nightclub in Towson. He was quiet, humble, and laconic—a hardworking Johnny Unitas type. She helped Larry study for a law degree and at 46 realized her own dream of becoming a lawyer.

My dad returned from Wheeling College in 1976 and got a job coaching the Johns Hopkins basketball team. He lived in the Guilford Manor apartments across from Homewood Field at

Hopkins, where on Sunday mornings the medical students would play a pick-up game of touch football in their scrubs. I often went down to the field, which was also deep centerfield of the baseball diamond, and played on one of the teams as an extra rusher. I'd count my four "Mississippis" and rush the passer.

The Colts were just starting to get good again. They had a young and dynamic quarterback from LSU named Bert Jones. He threw bombs to Roger Carr and Raymond Chester, and on third downs his favorite target was Don McCauley. Lydell Mitchell was a hard-nosed halfback who could catch the ball as well. The organization had cleaned house after Johnny Unitas left and the new players were beginning to gel. The defense was also getting better after a 4–10 season in 1973 and a 2–12 campaign in 1974.

In those losing years, most Colts home games did not sell out, and that meant they were not on television. Our lives hung on the crisp and poignant radio voices of Chuck Thompson and Vince Bagli. Thompson's voice, born from the concrete and splintered bleachers of Thirty-Third Street, transformed the exploits of the blue and white gladiators into legend. "Good afternoon everybody," he would boom from the transistor, and from that point on he was everybody's father. "When the ball was in motion, nobody described it better than Chuck," said Bagli. "We were a bunch of 'rinky-dinks' compared to him."

I witnessed two painful playoff defeats in Memorial Stadium. On December 19, 1976, my father took my brother and me to watch the AFC Divisional playoffs against the Steelers. The Colts had a rising star in Bert Jones and a defensive line called the Sack Pack, but their secondary was suspect. We sat in Uncle Buddy's seats in the horseshoe behind what was home plate during the baseball season. On the second play from scrimmage, Colts defensive lineman Joe Ehrmann broke through and tackled Franco Harris—putting him out of the postseason with an ankle injury.

On the next play, Terry Bradshaw dropped back to pass. My eyes traveled downfield before he threw the ball, and I could see a Steelers receiver down the far sideline alone—the nearest Colts defender 15 yards away. The play resulted in a 79-yard touchdown pass to Frank Lewis. The Colts never recovered and lost 40–14.

Just after the game had ended, a plane flown by the lunatic Donald Kroner crashed into the upper deck. Fans had left early because of the score and no one was hurt.

The next year, on Christmas Eve, I went with my Uncle Bernie to see the Oakland Raiders play the Colts in the playoffs. Carolyn Bartoli made us meatball subs and wrapped them in tinfoil. Kenny "The Snake" Stabler played quarterback for the Raiders that day, and they possessed many potent offensive weapons. It was an exciting back-and-forth contest—one of the greatest games in NFL history—but the Colts let it slip away.

We had the ball in the fourth quarter with a lead and a little over five minutes remaining. Instead of trying to get the first down, coach Ted Marchibroda—nicknamed "Furrowed Brow" by my Dad—called three straight running plays and had to punt the ball back to Oakland.

With 1:44 remaining and the Colts in the lead 31–28, Stabler dropped back to pass and threw a deep and lofting spiral to his tight end Dave Casper on a post route. As Casper went into the cut to the post, he looked back and saw the ball headed in the opposite direction over his right shoulder. He changed course in a writhing motion like a second baseman trying to flag down a pop-up being carried by the wind and somehow brought in the ball at the Colts' 14.

The Snake had reduced us to defenseless mice. That play, "The Ghost to the Post," allowed the Raiders to tie the game and eventually win in overtime, 37–31. My Uncle Bernie and I drove back to my grandmother's house in Parkville for our annual Christmas Eve celebration that included Nana's pasta and meatballs along with the turkey and stuffing.

It was my last Colts game. On the lot next to the house were the remaining rows of lonely Christmas trees left on a cold night. I went outside with a football and weaved my way through the trees on the lot like I was Lydell Mitchell scoring the game-winning touchdown against the Raiders. I spent a large part of my childhood changing the outcomes of Colts losses in my mind.

My brother and I moved from Baltimore to the suburbs of Chicago in 1979 to live with my mother and stepfather. Larry had been given an ultimatum from his company to take a promotion and relocate or never advance. It was one of the hardest things I've ever had to do.

My father stayed behind in Baltimore, along with the rest of my heroes—Unitas, Mackey, Mitchell, Jones, and Curtis. Our last dinner together was at the Flaming Pit, where my mother used to work. Dad gave me a blue blazer for my sixteenth birthday. My father was in tears and I could barely look at him. It was more gut-wrenching than when he had left for Wheeling. We took off for Chicago the next morning. The Colts never returned to the playoffs, and five years later owner Robert Irsay moved the team to Indianapolis. In my third year of college at the University of Virginia, I watched the devastating scene that ensued in Owings Mills as the snows came down and the Mayflower vans filled with all the Colts equipment, along with my childhood memories, departed.

One of my mother's friends on the North Shore of Chicago knew the Irsay family, and we got into a heated discussion about the Colts. Her name was Carry Buck, and her husband John was described to me by my mother as the Donald Trump of Chicago. His first job out of Notre Dame was to lease all the space in the Sears Tower. Mrs. Buck taught me my first lesson in business.

"It's his team, he can do what he wants with it," she said.

"I hate his guts," I said.

"That doesn't matter to him."

Soon thereafter, I also sold out to the Irsays. Carrie got me a job working for the Robert Irsay Heating and Cooling Company in Skokie, Illinois. It was a sweatshop filled with mastodon-like welders and tinners who spoke only in expletives, and I completed an assortment of odd jobs, including cleaning out trailers, many of which had Baltimore Colts stickers on them.

Football in Chicago was also a way of life, though the Bears weren't very good back then. Walter Payton was the star running back, and it seemed like he carried the ball on every play. Sometimes he even played quarterback. But compared to the glory days of the Baltimore Colts, the Bears were lumbering through their dark ages.

In truth, after the Colts left Baltimore, I lived in NFL exile for the next 12 years, only briefly adopting the Giants while living in Manhattan because I had played on punter Sean Landeta's basketball travel team when I was 10 years old. I could also justify being a Giants fan because their general manager George Young was also a Baltimorean. But I longed for the NFL to return to Baltimore and knew in my heart that I had no team.

When the Ravens arrived in Baltimore in 1996 from Cleveland, I was happy my city had a team but I didn't like the way it happened. I had attended graduate school in New York with novelist Michael Jaffe, a Browns fan who had frequented the Dawg Pound in Municipal Stadium. His passion for Cleveland matched any fan's passion for the Baltimore Colts. My city had sold our collective soul to get a team just the way Indianapolis had hijacked the Colts. It was hard to give them my heart.

My first Ravens game was against the Indianapolis Colts in 1998. Jim Harbaugh played quarterback for the Ravens, and it was Peyton Manning's rookie season. Ravens Stadium reminded me of those Coleco electronic football games with the vibrating fields that made the players move. There was no baseball diamond or dirt bowl like the old Memorial Stadium. The "Big Wheel" and the "Spoke" who ruled the upper deck at Colts games with their "C-O-L-T-S" cheer were also gone. The sidelines were narrow, making the field the main event.

I didn't know these people in the stands wearing purple jerseys with names like Boulware and Lewis. I didn't even know which team to root for, so I settled on cheering for the Ravens' Jim Harbaugh, whom I'd seen play for the Bears. The Colts had died inside me. Manning and Harbaugh dueled all afternoon, with the

Ravens prevailing, 38–31. It was the last time Peyton Manning lost in Baltimore as a Colt.

More than 30 years after holding her ears and running into her beauty shop during another Johnny Unitas comeback, Carolyn Bartoli attended her first Ravens game at the new stadium. The Ravens played the Vikings, and a lot of Minnesota fans in our section were dressed in helmets and shields, like Norse warriors. My friend Wayne Brokke, a Baltimore restaurant owner, had gotten the tickets and was attending his first football game. My grandmother fixed him with a Neapolitan eye and instructed him to "boo" whenever the Norse folk cheered for the Vikings and to cheer whenever they "booed."

At the age of 83, she witnessed three kickoff runbacks for touchdowns in the first quarter of the game, including two by the Ravens. Baltimore lost that game, but she talked about it for days. Nana made her delicacies on Sundays, and we watched the Ravens games at her home in Pasadena just as her brother and cousin had in the 1960s. Nana loved having football parties and turned the sound down so we could listen to Dean Martin's greatest hits like "You're Nobody till Somebody Loves You." Dino Bartoli still talked about Ameche and Marchetti.

I started taking an interest in the Ravens during the 2000 season. Ray Lewis had been charged with double murder in Atlanta the year before, and when he returned to the team after being acquitted he said he desperately needed to get to the Super Bowl.

During that year's playoffs, I watched from a hotel pool in Arizona as the Ravens played the Tennessee Titans. Tennessee had just missed winning the Super Bowl the year before by a couple of yards, but Baltimore was staying close to them in this game. Then Ray Lewis hit Titan running back Eddie George just as the ball arrived from quarterback Steve McNair. The Ravens' linebacker stole the ball and ran 50 yards for a touchdown. Game effectively over.

The next week Trent Dilfer found Shannon Sharpe on a slant pattern for a 92-yard touchdown against the Raiders. Tony Siragusa flattened Oakland quarterback Rich Gannon, and the Ravens were headed to Tampa for the Super Bowl. I watched the Ravens win the 2000 Super Bowl with my uncle, and we drove downtown after the game. People crowded the roads into the city. In Fells Point, fans climbed on street signs. I was happy for the city but I still didn't know these people.

A few months later I went to see *The Producers* on Broadway, starring Nathan Lane and Matthew Broderick. On the way to my seat, I saw Ravens owner Art Modell with Giants owner Wellington Mara, not quite the Leo Bloom and Max Bialystock of the NFL. I went up to Mr. Modell and introduced myself. "Thank you for bringing football back to Baltimore," I said. "My family members in Baltimore thank you."

"You're welcome," he said. "My pleasure."

I arrived at the Atlanta airport to discover that my connecting flight to New Orleans was delayed by an hour. The football gods were having a field day with me this Super Bowl Sunday. In the boarding area Ravens fans mixed with 49ers fans wearing Davis, Kaepernick, Gore, and Willis jerseys. Finally we took off and arrived in New Orleans shortly before 1:00 P.M. The atmosphere on Bourbon Street included packs of Ravens and 49ers fans. The Ravens mob drowned out the Niners faithful with Jack White's "Seven Nation Army" anthem. Niners fans struck back with Jim Harbaugh's popular refrain taken from his dad, "Who's got it better than us. No . . . body!"

It was football paradise. I never expected to be strolling down Bourbon Street waiting for my home team to play in the Super Bowl. I saw someone in full Johnny Unitas uniform—pads, jersey, high-top cleats. I thought about my son who had desperately wanted to go. He had recently played football for the first time in his life and was beginning to feel the pull of the game. He and I had fallen in love with these Ravens together.

I had moved my wife and two kids back to my hometown of Baltimore in August 2010 for a job at the Johns Hopkins University

Press. Shortly thereafter I scoured the classifieds for season tickets to the Ravens. I was struck by how passionate the city was for this team. It seemed that nearly everyone had exchanged Colts jerseys for Ravens garb. Game jerseys appeared everywhere around town on Purple Fridays.

Season tickets secured, we found a house close to my office at Hopkins. The stone mansion once occupied by the poet Ogden Nash, who immortalized the Colts in verse for a 1968 *Life* magazine article, stood just around the corner. My father had attended parties in the house next door to ours. That's Baltimore, or "Smalltimore" as it is called by the locals—a place where everyone is connected in some way.

At one time that house next door had belonged to the Fusting family, and my dad had gone to Loyola High School with Bill. In the late '50s, my house hadn't been built, and the lot was a long and flat rectangular patch where the Fusting boys played tackle football. I've described the scene in my poem "Trash Night":

The No. 11 bus to Canton
rounds the corner like Jim Parker,
and gone are the days of the Fusting boys
playing tackle on an empty lot
disguised as Unitas, Berry and Moore.

My 4-year-old son Quinn and I attended the first home game of the Ravens' 2010 season against the Cleveland Browns. The deafening sound in that stadium when the defense took the field made my son hold his ears. It's a roar that comes from the depths of the blast furnaces at Sparrow's Point, from the lathes and the printing presses and the abandoned locomotives parked just a few blocks away. Our seats are at the back of the end zone along Russell Street, where you can look out and see the roundhouse of the B&O train station and Pigtown to the west, the place where the stories from the television show *The Wire* unfold in real life every day. The intimate concrete bowl of the stadium fills with the agitated timbre of football fans chasing pigskin exploits from neighborhood to neighborhood—from Patterson Park to Homewood Field to the disenfranchised gridiron ghosts wandering Thirty-Third Street in search of Memorial Stadium.

It's the sound of Mobtown—with its roots in the Pratt Street riots at the onset of the Civil War and in the Battle of 1814, when the citizen-soldiers of the city repelled fleets of redcoats. My son and I became part of that tradition, but even so I still wasn't quite hooked.

On September 11, 2011, the Ravens opened at home against the Steelers, and I went with my father. I remembered that receiver Anquan Boldin had dropped a pass at the goal line in the last few minutes in Pittsburgh, a play that helped end the Ravens' 2010 season. It was the tenth anniversary of the World Trade Center tragedy and the ninth anniversary of Johnny Unitas's passing away.

My father and I walked down Martin Luther King Boulevard toward the stadium. He had once told me, "I'm a fan as long as they don't embarrass the city." We both wore Ravens jerseys; it was the first game with the new franchise that we had ever attended together. The Ravens demolished the Steelers 35–7. Ray Rice took the first snap and blasted through the hole for 36 yards into Pittsburgh territory. Two plays later, Boldin snared a 27-yard touchdown pass. And then something strange happened. The referee raised his arms and mistakenly announced, "Baltimore Colts touchdown!" It was an unintentional nod to Unitas and all the former Baltimore Colts who had embraced the Ravens, old friends like Lenny Moore and Bruce Laird.

I looked at my dad in his Ray Lewis jersey and thought of his 60 years of following football in Baltimore. In that moment I became a Ravens fan.

In the fall of 2012, I coached my daughter Julia's grade school soccer team. We played our home games on that field off Rogers Avenue where the Colts had practiced on a late August day in 1970. It's now called Northwest Park, and I often wondered if I was the only one who had experienced its storied past. I may have been the only parent who knew that the barn-like gymnasium on the side of the hill was once called the Bees' Nest.

During the games, I would turn around and look at those wooden plank bleachers, overgrown with grass. In my mind I saw Mike Curtis carry John Unitas on his shoulders up the steps one more time.

I've spent my life running under a Unitas touchdown pass.

1. No Huddle, No Defense

The suited up boys
practice in rows, repeated
runs at the sled . . .
watching the game
on the field, you almost forget
the effort required, plays
practiced in pieces,
finally whole.

—JANE SATTERFIELD

I WALKED SLOWLY with the crowd to M&T Bank Stadium, passing through Oriole Park on Monday evening, September 10, for the first Ravens game of the year against the Bengals. Something was different. The Orioles, perennial basement dwellers for more than a decade, were still very much alive in a fight for the American League East Division title. For the first time in 14 years, the Birds had unfinished business in September. As a Baltimore sports fan, I didn't know if I was in a purple haze or an orange crush.

In previous seasons, the Ravens had dominated the discussion on Baltimore sports talk radio as early as June. This time, the start of the 2012 Ravens season was a much needed and comparatively relaxing diversion from the tension-packed innings and the promise of playoff baseball, even though the dull pain from the AFC Championship loss still lingered like an aching joint before the rain. This year's schedule had many predicting that a 9–7 record would be a realistic expectation, with home games against New England, Dallas, the New York Giants, and Denver, and on the road in Houston and also in San Diego, where the Ravens had been handily defeated by the Chargers the year before.

I wore my Torrey Smith Ravens jersey and a throwback Orioles cap from the late '70s with the cartoon bird against a white panel. Countless others did the same. Combining Ravens and Orioles gear would become, from this day's home opener to Bourbon Street and the Super Bowl, the new uniform for Baltimore, honoring the winged warriors of both teams.

Inside the stadium, Orioles Matt Wieters, Adam Jones, J. J. Hardy, and Buck Showalter were on hand to cheer on the Ravens as they prepared to face the Cincinnati Bengals. The crowd erupted when their faces appeared on the big screen.

In honor of his dominating performance in the London Olympics, swimmer Michael Phelps ran out of the tunnel with the offense wearing a number 12 Ravens jersey with "Phelps" on the back and took part in the official coin toss. Phelps had won 22 medals, 18 of them gold, and the jersey number he chose was a nod to the newest Raven, Jacoby Jones. Phelps had started following the Ravens in 1996, when he was 11 and the team moved to Baltimore.

With a bevy of sports figures in attendance, including Muhammad Ali, homage was now paid to the man who had brought football back to the city. The crowd observed a moment of silence for former owner Art Modell, who had died of natural causes on the previous Thursday, September 6. Ravens executives and players, including Ozzie Newsome, Steve Bisciotti, Kevin Byrne, John Harbaugh, and Ray Lewis, had visited his bedside in the final hours. Newsome held his hand and whispered, "I want you to know what good hands feel like," according to *The Byrne Identity* blog.

Ray Lewis wore the initials A. M. across his eye black in honor of the owner who had supported him throughout his 17-year career—through Pro Bowl seasons and bad decisions made off the field. He told *USA Today*, "I genuinely loved Art as a man, and he showed me what to strive for in life. When you truly see the impact he had on everyone he touched, it humbles you."

While being mourned in Baltimore, Modell was being excoriated in Cleveland, the city from which he had moved the Ravens. A comedian joked, "The season hasn't started and we're already 1–0." The passing of the owner, who had joined the NFL in 1961 when he bought the Browns for $4 million, reopened old wounds. What Robert Irsay is to Baltimore for moving the beloved Colts to Indianapolis, Modell became to Cleveland when he brought the old Browns to Maryland and renamed them the Ravens.

"I visited Art Modell every year in the owners' suite in Baltimore," tweeted former Titans and Ravens wide receiver Derrick Mason after hearing the news. "He was never [the] same after moving the Browns. I believe it broke his heart."

The Ravens unveiled jersey patches for his passing that displayed "Art" in white letters against a circular black background. In a different sense, Ravens football "art" over the past three years had been more the drop splatter drip technique of Jackson Pollock than the smooth edges of an Edward Hopper.

During the 2011 season, the team had created a masterpiece one week and entered a blue period the next. After blowing out the Steelers in the opening game, the next week they crashed in Tennessee and lost to a bad Titans team. Losses to weak teams like the Titans and Jaguars had destined them to play the Patriots on the road in New England for the AFC Championship, a fate that may well have tilted an agonizingly close game toward defeat.

With the 2012 kickoff moments away, Ray Lewis's team faced lingering issues on both sides of the ball. It was still Ray's team, at least for one more year, and he had challenged his teammates in Foxborough at the end of last season to "get back to work." The defense was old and vulnerable without Terrell Suggs, who had injured his ankle. The offense remained under scrutiny, with questions swirling around offensive coordinator Cam Cameron and quarterback Joe Flacco.

In the off-season, the embattled coordinator had implemented a "no-huddle" offense to instill a sense of urgency and keep opposing defenses on their heels. The 2011 offense had lacked a killer instinct, and the heat was on Cameron. His detractors argued that bland offensive schemes had held Flacco back, relying too much on generic pass routes and low-risk throws. In the early years of his career in Baltimore, Flacco had simply managed games and wasn't asked to carry the team by creating something out of nothing.

Fans had grown impatient and wanted to see the reins loosened. There was speculation that the relationship between Cameron and Flacco had become strained, and Joe's body language as he slowly came to the line on certain plays suggested that maybe he didn't agree with the calls. Owner Steve Bisciotti had ratcheted up the pressure on his offensive coordinator:

"Everybody who is trying to be great is going to be scrutinized, and most people that are great rise above it and use it for motivation," he said. "I think Cam is one of those people." Bisciotti had said after the 2010 season in the *Baltimore Sun*, "We like Cam under fire as our coordinator next year."

The Ravens had employed a hurry-up style with success against the Patriots in the 2011 playoffs and in a last-second victory at Pittsburgh during the regular season. Comfortable in the shotgun formation since his days at the University of Delaware, Flacco finally had what he wanted. "I love the no-huddle," the normally reserved Flacco told ESPN. "We've got to get quicker and quicker at it. That's what we are going to be."

Joe's performance against New England in the AFC Championship kept the Flacco bashers at bay for the moment. According to the message boards and out-of-town call-in shows, Joe was good enough to make it to a Super Bowl, but he was not a top-five quarterback.

It was said that he didn't read his progressions fast enough and resorted to his check-down receivers too quickly. Flacco could lead an offense down the field with ease at times and then struggle. He could loft a beautiful touch pass into a tight window in the corner of the end zone for a touchdown and fumble in the next series. He didn't play like the league's precision passing machines: Drew Brees, Tom Brady, Peyton Manning, and Aaron Rodgers. "The criticism was mind-boggling at times," said Bob Haynie, sports talk radio host in Baltimore. "Everyone wants that QB on the commercials who puts up big fantasy numbers."

While attempting to negotiate a new contract in the off-season, Flacco stoked the coals with a bold statement regarding his status as an elite quarterback. "I mean, I think I'm the best. I don't think I'm top five, I think I'm the best. I don't think I'd be very successful at my job if I didn't feel that way," he told Baltimore's WNST 1570 in April 2012.

Criticized for being too laid back, the soft-spoken signal caller was now being chided for his audacity. None of it fazed him. Even in praising himself, his humble demeanor prevailed when he used the word "think" four times. He turned down a contract that would have paid him $14.9 million per year, opting to play out the season for a potentially much bigger payday.

There were also concerns about a recent drop in his production and the need to increase his touchdown passes in 2012—mostly driven by the statistics-crazed fantasy set. He had thrown 25 in 2010 and only 20 in 2011. In response, one message board participant wrote: "The only thing Flacco needs to raise this season is the Lombardi Trophy."

The offense had received upgrades before the season started. In March, general manager Ozzie Newsome and his staff added another weapon, a fast wide receiver and kick returner from the Houston Texans named Jacoby Jones. They also bolstered the coaching staff by signing Jim Caldwell, former head coach of the Indianapolis Colts, to become the Ravens quarterbacks coach. While Flacco had played well under the tutelage of previous quarterbacks coach Jim Zorn, Caldwell had taken the Indianapolis Colts to a Super Bowl in 2009 and had mentored Peyton Manning before replacing Tony Dungy as head coach. Caldwell's calm demeanor seemed a good match for Flacco's personality.

The defense, for one of the few times in franchise history, was projected to be worse than the offense. The loss of star linebacker Terrell Suggs in January to an Achilles tendon injury after one of the best seasons in his career in 2011 and the salary cap casualties of top performers Cory Redding and fan favorite Jarret Johnson threatened to cripple the unit. With "T-Sizzle" out for at least six games, linebackers Dannell Ellerbe, Jameel McClain, and Paul Kruger needed to step up their play to make up for the loss.

Eccentric All-Pro safety Ed Reed—he of the acrobatic interceptions and unkempt goatee—added to the uncertainty when he publicly speculated about whether or not he would play in 2012. In May, he told Sirius XM radio show host Adam Schein that he wasn't 100 percent sure he would return for another season, citing safety issues from all the hits given and received in a decade in the league and a desire to spend more time with his son.

Ray Lewis provided the necessary cover for his longtime sidekick by saying that nothing had changed in Reed's preparation and predicted his fellow future Hall of Famer would be there. When training camp started, Reed was with the team.

Once the players lined up for the kickoff of a new season and the crowd began their "Seven Nation Army" cheer ("WOAH-OH-OH-OH-OH . . . OH") adopted from the opening riff of the White Stripes song, the football season had started. The Orioles' chase for their first playoff spot in 14 years would have to wait until Tuesday night.

On the first play from scrimmage against the Bengals, Joe Flacco answered his critics with a 52-yard bomb off a play fake down the middle to Torrey Smith. The bold move sent a message to the fan base that this season was going to be different than last year. Justin Tucker, the rookie from Texas who beat Billy Cundiff out for the kicking job, gave the Ravens a 3–0 lead.

Then Ray Rice rushed for a touchdown, and Flacco found Anquan Boldin on a 34-yard strike, throwing off his back foot to the receiver, who crashed into the end zone with two defenders on top of him. The Ravens built an early 17–3 lead.

The Bengals scored a late-first-half touchdown to trail by only 7 points. Quarterback Andy Dalton tried a sneak on third down from the Ravens' 10-yard line in the middle of the third quarter and was stopped just short of the goal line. The Bengals trailed by only 4 points, 17–13, and fans in my section, at the back of the end zone, were getting queasy.

On the next drive Flacco targeted tight end Dennis Pitta and Ray Rice on successive pass plays to move the ball into Cincinnati territory. After an 18-yard pass to Ed Dickson, Flacco threw a "jump ball" to Pitta, who went up and took it away from two Bengals defenders for a touchdown. The Ravens stopped the Bengals on the next drive and added a field goal to lead 27–13. Then the defense went to work.

The greatest defensive centerfielder to ever play baseball in Baltimore was Paul Blair. He played for the Orioles in the golden years from 1964 through 1976, and won eight Gold Gloves, including a string of seven in a row. When I was growing up, Blair was my favorite Oriole. I learned how to catch fly balls by copying his quick and stealthy style of playing shallow and breaking back on balls with sudden bursts of speed. On this day, sitting in a Ravens luxury box in the first game of 2012, current Orioles centerfielder Adam Jones was about to witness the exploits of an extraordinary outfielder of a different kind—one who shagged line drives and fly balls of the pigskin variety on a football field.

Football's best centerfielder for the past decade has been Ed Reed. The aging scholar of the game continued to roam the secondary and dare any quarterback to throw in his direction. He had terrorized Tom Brady and Peyton Manning for most of their careers. It didn't matter who was taking snaps, and young quarterbacks were especially susceptible. He studied tendencies and knew formations. At times he gambled and took unnecessary risks—like ill-conceived laterals that wound up in the hands of the other team—all part of his aggressive nature. When the opposition made a big play and one of Reed's protégés like Chykie Brown or Cary Williams was responsible, you would see Reed's helmet shake in disapproval or his fingers touch the side of his head.

Ray Lewis controlled the team in the locker room and in the pregame huddle, but in his quiet way Reed led by example on the field. Even in the twilight of his career, on opening night in 2012, he altered the course of the game.

Reed got inside Andy Dalton's head and put the game out of reach for the Bengals. Down 27–13 at the end of the third quarter, Dalton took a shot by going deep to A. J. Green, a pass that went incomplete. On third and nine, he threw into the right flat underneath the coverage, but the ball sailed on him. Reed sensed it and broke toward the ball, catching it below his knees and stumbling forward toward the goal line for 34 yards and a touchdown.

At about the 7-yard line, Reed held the ball out and as he soared toward the goal line headed out of bounds. At the last possible second, he extended the ball over the pylon and the referee signaled "touchdown." The Bengals were done, but the Ravens put up 10 more points to start the season with an emphatic win, 44–13. Flacco finished with an impressive 21–29 for 299 yards and two touchdowns. The official debut of the no-huddle offense erased any doubts at least for a week.

Cincinnati moved the ball with ease into Ravens territory during the game but scored only one touchdown. The Bengals had gouged the Ravens defense for 323 yards of total offense. In the first game of the year, a theme had emerged for the 2012 Ravens. Their "red zone" defense had flummoxed Cincinnati and would develop a resilient and unrivaled stinginess when it came to giving up touchdowns.

The Ravens defense demonstrated this new personality trait again in stopping the Eagles' opening drive the next week in Philadelphia. Michael Vick drove straight down the field deep into Ravens territory. On second and 9 from the Ravens' 12, Vick scrambled and threw across the field. Safety Bernard Pollard switched direction, diving across the field to make an interception and keep the Eagles out of the end zone. With the score tied 7–7 and the Eagles on the Ravens' 20, Albert McClellan recovered a Michael Vick fumble, and another red zone stop resulted in a momentum shift for Baltimore.

On the next two plays, Ray Rice ran for 43 yards and Flacco connected on a 21-yard strike to Jacoby Jones to give the Ravens a 14–7 lead. The Ravens stuffed the Eagles again inside the Baltimore 10-yard line. Cornerback Lardarius Webb forced a fumble that was recovered by Ray Lewis. Baltimore led 17–7 at halftime.

In the second half, the Ravens offense stalled. After running the no-huddle 22 times against the Bengals, they used it for only six plays against the Eagles. Ray Rice had gained 78 of his 99 yards in the first half, but had only nine touches in the second half.

Joe Flacco's performance in the first quarter was impeccable, but he reverted to the inconsistency that had plagued him in previous seasons for the rest of the game, going only 8 for 25 in the second half. There were six short-yardage situations in the game, and the Ravens threw on all of them.

The last two came with Baltimore on the move with a little over a minute left. Inside Eagle territory on the 46, they needed only 1 yard for a first down trailing 24–23. On third down, Flacco threw incomplete to the sideline for Pitta. He tried to connect with Rice on the opposite sideline, and it sailed over his head. The game was over.

Questions arose immediately over the play calling. "We thought about running the ball, yeah, but we thought we had some good calls," said Harbaugh afterward in quotes published by *USA Today*. "I think that's fair. You could have called a draw or something there, but you know they were bringing some heat, and they were hugging the backs too. It would have been hit or miss." It had been an emotional game for the Ravens coach, who had returned to the city where he had spent 10 years as special teams coordinator and secondary coach under Andy Reid.

The defense gave up 486 yards of total offense but forced three turnovers inside the "red zone" or the Eagles would have blown out the Ravens. In the end, tight end Brent Celek had tallied eight catches for 157 yards, and DeSean Jackson had caught seven balls for 114 yards. LeSean McCoy had rushed for 85 yards. The Eagles would go on to win only 4 games the entire 2012 season against 12 defeats—their worst showing since 1998.

This was also the first game in which the Ravens experienced the negative effects of replacement officials. The regular NFL officials had been in a labor dispute with the league over their retirement plans and salaries. The lockout began in June, and negotiations had been ongoing. The replacements included officials from lower college divisions, the arena football league, and the lingerie football league.

The Ravens believed the substitute refs had robbed them of a key fumble recovery and a touchdown in the fourth quarter when Jacoby Jones and defensive back Nnamdi Asomugha went up for a ball and incidental contact was made. Asomugha wasn't playing the ball and didn't know where it was. Jones reached up and brought down the pass. He was called for offensive pass interference.

The touchdown would have given the Ravens a 10-point lead with five minutes remaining in the fourth quarter. Instead of throwing a yellow flag, the ref tossed a blue beanie onto the field, evoking scenes from Abbott and Costello. "They talk about the integrity of the game," Flacco said of the NFL during the postgame press conference, "and I think this is along those lines. The fact that we don't have the normal guys out there is pretty crazy." Flacco's postgame comments about the replacement refs impressed *Sports Illustrated*'s Peter King, who subsequently wrote that the Ravens had gotten the worst of the refs in the second week of the season.

The NFL kept the replacements on the field for another week while they remained in negotiations with the real officials. Then the Green Bay Packers lost to Seattle on a Hail Mary pass when receiver Golden Tate was awarded a touchdown that he didn't catch and that should have been ruled an interception. Defensive backs all over the league seized the moment and interfered with receivers. It was like a classroom with substitute teachers who did not know the curriculum and couldn't control the students. In what ultimately amounted to only three weeks of work, the flurry of penalties they called and the ensuing confusion affected teams equally.

But there were no excuses. The Eagles game had been a winnable one and revealed all the preseason concerns with the Ravens. The offense went into hibernation, and an aging defense gave up close to 500 yards of total offense to a team that barely defeated the Cleveland Browns the week before.

The statistics were disturbing considering what lay ahead for the 2012 Ravens. Michael Vick, a quarterback on the downside of his career, passed for 371 yards. Brent Celek racked up 157 yards in receptions. What would New England's Tom Brady and tight end Rob Gronkowski do to the Ravens defense in the next game? The stage was set for a grudge match with the Patriots, who had benefited from the Ravens' self-destructive tendencies in last year's AFC Championship game.

Scenes from the Ravens' loss had continued to haunt me through the off-season. On a Saturday evening in April 2012, when the University of Maryland played Johns Hopkins in a sold-out game at the Yankee Stadium of lacrosse, Homewood Field on the Hopkins campus, I took my kids to see it. I have a strong connection to lacrosse—during the 1970s, I had witnessed several classic battles between the two best programs in the country when my dad coached basketball at Hopkins.

When we arrived at the home-team side of the field, Ravens coach John Harbaugh and Patriots head coach Bill Belichick were having a discussion at the fence behind the Hopkins bench. I wondered how they could be so casual together after such a gut-wrenching game the previous January. I didn't know then that they were friends and that Belichick had recommended Harbaugh for the Ravens job in 2008. In fact, Belichick's career had helped shape the Baltimore Ravens' first Super Bowl victory in 2001.

As Browns head coach in 1995, Belichick had ensured that the Ravens would have a second first-round pick in the 1996 draft based on a previous trade he'd made. If he hadn't secured it, Ray Lewis would not have become a Raven. The team had selected Jonathan Ogden with their own first-round pick and fourth overall in the draft. Lewis came later in the first round with the pick Belichick had traded for. Belichick had also mentored Ozzie Newsome in matters related to the draft. "Ozzie gives Bill a lot of credit for his success," said Ravens senior vice president Kevin Byrne.

As a kid growing up in Annapolis, Belichick attended a lot of Hopkins lacrosse games. "He's an Annapolitan," said Hopkins coach Dave Pietramala, and "he loves Hopkins lacrosse and is committed to excellence like us." Pietramala had named a film study room for the coach in their new $10 million lacrosse facility, still under construction at the southeast end of the stadium.

Belichick's connection to the Baltimore area represented stability for him. His dad coached at Navy for 33 years, but prior to that the family had traveled around the coaching circuit. Young Billy started writing scouting reports at the age of nine and served as a gopher for Colts coach Ted Marchibroda at now-demolished Memorial Stadium, only seven blocks from Hopkins.

He had worked for both Robert Irsay in Baltimore and Art Modell in Cleveland, and he is one of the greatest coaches in the history of the NFL, defying the limitations of salary caps and the league's preference that one team not dominate all others every year.

I watched his conversation with Harbaugh and remembered my own childhood, when the day after a game my dad and I would go over stat sheets smeared in pizza grease from the postgame meal he shared with other coaches on nearby Greenmount Avenue. I had wanted to be a college basketball coach with my father, but it didn't turn out that way.

On that night at a lacrosse game, I gained more insight into the Patriots coach and sensed what he had experienced growing up. I also suspected he understood that the Ravens had outplayed his Patriots last January.

As the Terrapins packed the goal with their fierce defense and frustrated the Blue Jays the entire night, I thought of the final sequence in the AFC Championship game one last time. On second and 1 from the New England 14-yard line with 22 seconds remaining and down 23–20 in the 2011 AFC Championship game, Joe Flacco took a short drop and expertly delivered a bullet to wide receiver Lee Evans. It was a perfectly thrown ball, right into Evans's number 83 on his jersey. Flacco had made some remarkable throws in the game and had outplayed Tom Brady. He threw for more yards than Brady and completed two touchdowns passes to Brady's none.

Lee Evans caught the ball for a split second, and the arms of Ravens fans went into the air signaling "touchdown" at neighborhood parties and barrooms all around Baltimore. The standing-room-only crowds at Roman's, the Dizz, the Charles Village Pub, and the Swallow at the Hollow erupted. Evans turned as his second foot came down, and Patriot defensive back Sterling Moore, activated from the practice squad only a few days prior, suddenly stripped the ball before Evans's foot touched end zone turf. In one instant, the Ravens were headed to the Super Bowl. In another, Evans had dropped the ball, and the Ravens had fallen a fingernail short of victory.

A former Buffalo Bill, Evans had joined the Ravens during the preseason after they released Derrick Mason. During a 34–31 Bills overtime loss in Baltimore in 2010, Evans had caught six balls for 105 yards and three touchdowns. But in Cam Cameron's offense, Evans had only four catches the entire season before Flacco called his number against the Patriots.

Where was Lee Evans turning to go after he caught the ball? Why didn't he collapse and fall down backward into the end zone with both arms around the ball? Was he going to run across the back of the end zone and celebrate? Was he trying to get away from Sterling Moore? The questions had played in my mind for months.

Two plays later, Billy Cundiff missed a chip-shot 32-yard field goal to tie the game. The ball came off his foot and veered to the left of the goalpost. "A collective sense of utter despair as the season comes to an end," said Ravens announcer Gerry Sandusky.

"The Evans 'drop,' though devastating in that a catch would have likely led to a victory, was more acceptable than the Cundiff missed field goal," said Mark Viviano, sports director of WJZ-TV in Baltimore. "Patriots cornerback Sterling Moore made an excellent defensive play though Evans still should have secured the catch. Credit the defense. There's no excuse for the missed field goal that at least would've sent the game to overtime."

Ray Lewis watched the kick sail wide, and he picked up his helmet and walked off the field without reaction. The defense had done its job and had put the offense in a position to win the game.

On the series before, the great New England quarterback had needed just one first down to win the game. Brady walked to the line facing a third and 4 from his own 39. In the defensive play of the year for the Ravens, safety Ed Reed deflected a 4-yard pass away from the elusive Aaron Hernandez to give his team a chance to win the game. Hernandez was a cinch to make that catch against most if not all defensive backs in the NFL, and if he had, the game would have been over and the Patriots could have begun to celebrate on the sidelines.

But Ed Reed just would not let that happen. He had seen the play on film and replayed it a hundred times before. That's why his coaches made him captain as a sophomore at the University of Miami. He was born to read defenses and was covering Hernandez as only he could, and he knew the exact route he was going to run. Tom Brady had written on his wristband, "Find number 20 on every play."

The Ravens defense had delivered another outstanding performance. The Patriots committed three turnovers and were held to under 100 yards rushing. Brady had turned in a pedestrian performance with only 239 yards in the air. At the end of his 16th season, Ray Lewis, in search of one more trip to the Super Bowl, managed to keep the moment in perspective.

"I was at Ray Lewis's locker following the loss, and it was quite remarkable how calm he was and how protective he was of both Cundiff and Evans—repeating that no one play is to blame in a loss," said Viviano. "Lewis kept repeating, 'It just wasn't our time.' I found that remarkable given that Ray Lewis's chances of getting to another Super Bowl were about up."

In the locker room video from the Ravens Web site, Lewis huddled together with his team. "It ain't about one play, it ain't about nothing. This year we did what we were supposed to do. . . . And the fact is, we gotta come back and go to work to make sure we finish it next time. That's all we gotta do."

Lewis spoke like a father to his sons and singled out a quarterback who had just played the best game of his career. "Joe, you played your ass off. . . . Don't ever . . . don't ever drop your head when you're coming through a loss. Because there's too much pain outside of here that people are really going through."

Joe Flacco had played poorly in the second half of the loss to the Philadelphia Eagles in 2012's second game. He had a solid track record since 2008 for showing up in big games, but still it seemed unlikely that he could outperform Tom Brady again, even at home.

Arriving at the Ravens' stadium on Sunday night, September 23, 2012, I learned through word of mouth about another death in the Ravens family. Tevin Jones, the 19-year-old brother of receiver Torrey Smith, had died in a motorcycle crash in Northern Virginia late Saturday night. Smith had been a father figure to Tevin and his eight other siblings. The second-year receiver decided to play in the game. "I can't believe my little brother is gone," he tweeted. "Be thankful for your loved ones and tell them you love them . . . this is the hardest thing ever."

Tom Brady started strong and moved the Patriots down the field at will. He stood tall in the saddle, and watching him in person for the first time, I was amazed at his ability to see the whole field. He drove the offense like a signal tower on wheels, transmitting passes to Wes Welker and Brandon Lloyd with preset signals. He would bring the team to the line, assess the defense, and steer his offense away from Lewis and Reed. On the running plays he would determine where the soft spots existed in the coverage, then burn the Ravens on the next play with a pass. The Patriots averaged only 2.2 yards per rush in the game and were deliberate in their execution, passing for 10 to 15 yards at a time. Brady picked on cornerback Cary Williams repeatedly throughout the game. The Ravens defense allowed two field goals and one touchdown in the first quarter and trailed 13–0 to the 2012 AFC champions. The offense meanwhile had not yet recorded a first down.

In the second quarter, Flacco struck back using a combination of Ray Rice, Dennis Pitta, Anquan Boldin, and Torrey Smith. On a first down from the Patriots' 25-yard line, Flacco threw deep into the corner of the end zone. As he crossed the goal line, Smith bumped his defender and went airborne to catch the ball that put the Ravens on the board. The play altered the momentum of the game and helped catapult the Ravens into the lead, 14–13. Brady marched right back down the field and found Julian Edelman for a 7-yard touchdown strike. The Patriots led 20–13 at halftime.

During halftime, my seat neighbor Butch Wilson and I talked about the AFC Championship game and Billy Cundiff's missed field goal. "It wasn't that boy's fault," said Butch with genuine concern. "He was rushed onto the field. I blame that one on Harbaugh. He needed to call a timeout. They mismanaged that game."

Butch works as a pipefitter for the Coast Guard at a shipyard in Curtis Bay south of the city. His use of the term "boy" revealed a nuance that is intrinsic to the city's worship of its athletes.

In Baltimore, we all belonged to the same extended football family. It started with the Colts and their presence in our neighborhoods and grocery stores, and it has carried over to the Ravens regardless of the fact that today's players are largely unapproachable and cordoned off by their corporate handlers. The Colts made it easy for us because many of them stayed in the city after they retired.

"We had it better than anyone playing in Baltimore," said beloved Colts defensive lineman Artie Donovan. "The city saved my life. I would have been dead long ago as a cop living in New York."

The pain of the Patriots loss and the missed field goal was still fresh in Butch's eyes. Cundiff and his struggles were ours to own, and Butch cared for the kicker's well-being. He was also worried about the Patriots in this game and our ability to stop Brady. The defense had looked vulnerable in the first half. "This one's going down to the wire," he said. "We've got a long way to go if the defense is going to play like this. They miss Suggs real bad."

The second half resembled a boxing match, with each offense moving the ball at will. Torrey Smith made two big catches in the opening drive of the third quarter, including one for 32 yards, and Ray Rice powered the ball into the end zone for a Ravens lead, 21–20.

A dozen plays later, the Patriots surged ahead 27–21. After the Ravens failed to convert a fourth and 1 from the Patriots' 33 with 10 minutes left in the fourth, Brady moved his team into field goal position again to extend the lead, 30–21.

Flacco responded with a 5-yard touchdown pass to a falling-down Torrey Smith, and the Ravens trailed 30–28. Smith would end the game with 117 receiving yards. The game came down to the defense needing a stop, and they got one. Bernard Pollard defended Rob Gronkowski on a third and 16, and the pass was broken up. Gronkowski, the Patriots tight end, had been completely shut down in the game. The Ravens' game plan had dictated that he was not going to beat them, and they held him to two catches for 22 yards.

The Ravens got the ball back with less than two minutes remaining, and Flacco nailed six of seven passes for 72 yards. Jacoby Jones came up big with a 24-yard catch and a pass interference penalty that moved the game-winning kick 10 yards closer for Justin Tucker.

The new kicker had an opportunity to win an important game for his team that would provide a fresh start from the wreckage of the 2011 AFC Championship game. The kick barely nudged inside the right upright. As it rose above the right goalpost, the ball was almost directly on top of it. Ten yards farther away and the kick would have missed.

Patriots nose tackle Vince Wilfork tore off his helmet and pleaded his case to the replacement officials that the kick was "no good." Bill Belichick did the same as time ran out, even grabbing an official by the arm. The travesty of the replacement refs had almost ruined the game. They called 24 penalties in all and 14 against the Ravens.

In the first three weeks of the season, the Ravens had dealt with and overcome many of the lingering problems that had vexed them in 2011 and still had the chance to win all three games. It had been an emotional three weeks, and a 2–1 record positioned them for the road ahead. Torrey Smith had honored his deceased brother by catching two touchdown passes in the Ravens' victory over the Patriots. They had survived the replacement officials and had begun to even a score against a team that had kept them from the Super Bowl the year before. Joe Flacco had bested Tom Brady for the second straight game, throwing for three touchdowns to Brady's one. In the end, the Ravens defense had kept the game's most prolific and dominating offense out of the end zone and had forced them to settle for three field goals in addition to three touchdowns. It was a risky playing style and one that wouldn't win many beauty contests, but it suited the personnel of the 2012 Ravens perfectly. "Our team just fights," said John Harbaugh at the press conference.

Both the offense and defense of the Ravens had shown new wrinkles in the first few weeks of the season, but there weren't any major adjustments or departures from 2011. While it gave Cam Cameron some buzz and cover in the preseason, the no-huddle offense was really just a hurry-up two-minute drill that was used at different points of the game. It made their late-game comeback attempts against Philly and New England sharper and more routine. One year older in the NFL, they were a veteran ball club that relied on the experience and knowledge of their older players to win games.

The defense was not what it had been in the 2000s when it ranked in the top five for nearly a decade. Far from it—they now allowed teams to march at will between the 20-yard lines. But then the mind game with Ray Lewis and Ed Reed began. They guarded the goal line with ferocity and made it difficult for opposing offenses to score touchdowns.

Harbaugh went on to say, "What would be a better story than the one you saw?"

After beating the Patriots and with 13 difficult games ahead of them, Ray Lewis and the rest of the Baltimore Ravens stayed focused on the one possible ending that would go far beyond beating New England.

2. Never Easy, Never Pretty

. . . wired to the ball
I turn in step with its arc . . .
flying towards intercept.

—Doug Storm

THREE GAMES into the season, the 2012 Ravens had begun sculpting an identity that differed from any Ravens team that had come before them. They had dealt with the loss of former owner Art Modell and Torrey Smith's brother Tevin Jones, who had died in a motorcycle crash. They had destroyed a formidable division rival in the Bengals and beaten one of the premiere NFL franchises in the Patriots. They had won and lost close games by a single point.

The Ravens faced the Cleveland Browns, the Kansas City Chiefs, and the Dallas Cowboys in their next three games. Each of these opponents tested the mettle of a Ravens team that could no longer dominate physically and win street fights in the alleyways of offensive and defensive lines. And they survived. In these games, the Ravens demonstrated a preference for ugly wins—the more grotesque the better.

After a hideous 9–6 win in Kansas City that would have been a loss if the hapless Chiefs hadn't fumbled the ball on first and goal from the Ravens' 1-yard line, John Harbaugh yelled in the locker room as loud as he could, "Such a great win! The defense got one more stop! The offense got one more first down!"

The Ravens looked horrid for stretches and like champions as time ran out. They gave up long drives and big plays but shut down the end zone. They'd disappear for quarters at a time and come back to gouge out victories when it counted. But they had put into practice a lesson learned after the 2011 AFC Championship loss in Foxborough about the game of football. The next play counted more than the one that came before it, and the only thing that mattered at the end of any game was what the scoreboard said.

Four days after the Ravens defeated the Patriots in a close game, 31–30, they met the Cleveland Browns in Baltimore on Thursday night, September 27, 2013. They were playing their fourth game in 18 days to start the season.

The NFL had reached agreement with the regular referees, who were back on the job. In their absence the Ravens had been the fifth-most-penalized team, and they were pleased to see the first-string referees back in action. One fan held up a sign that read: "Finally! We get to yell at real refs! Welcome back!"

Dating back to 2008, the Ravens had won eight straight games against the Browns and held a 21–7 advantage since the "new" Browns had rejoined the NFL in 1999. The Browns had compiled a 73–151 record since returning to the NFL as an expansion franchise after Art Modell moved the team to Baltimore. There had been five different coaches in 13 years and many bad draft picks, such as quarterbacks Tim Couch and Brady Quinn, as well as others that never panned out.

During the most recent Ravens winning streak against Cleveland, the games had been classic tussles with each team's physicality on display. The Browns had been rebuilding a physical, Ravens-like team to compete in the AFC North, and they were getting closer to achieving that goal. In 2010, my son Quinn and

I watched Peyton Hillis run over the Ravens for 144 yards. The Browns led by 3 in Baltimore late before the Ravens came back to win the game, 24–17.

Every time the Browns played the Ravens, I thought about the move from Cleveland and the loss of the Colts. I had convinced myself that Cleveland had kept their name and that going 12 years without a franchise was far worse than anything the Browns fans had endured.

In retrospect, our good fortune in Baltimore had far surpassed the preservation of the nomenclature. We got rid of a drunken lunatic in Robert Irsay, who would have been a toxic force had he stayed under any circumstance. We fared far better in the long run than Browns fans, whose team and organization continued to simmer in the pyres of the Cuyahoga River.

After two expansion franchises went to Charlotte and Jacksonville in 1993, people like former Colts bandleader John Ziemann became incensed at NFL Commissioner Paul Tagliabue. "It was clear to us that he didn't want Baltimore to have another team. We deserved it over Jacksonville." The mood in town had become desperate. "I'll always believe that the NFL allowed Irsay to take the name because they never thought we'd get another team."

Connections were made with Modell and the Browns in the decade before the move. Ziemann's Colts Marching Band had played in Cleveland during the years that Baltimore didn't have an NFL team. "They liked us because we were cheap," Ziemann said. "They invited us back every year and introduced us to other teams."

Former Colts halfback Tom Matte, who had enlisted the advice of his old friend Art Modell about a Canadian Football League team he was helping to bring to Baltimore, had also spoken with him about bringing the Browns to Charm City.

"Art and I came into the league together in 1961," Matte said. "I had grown up in Cleveland rooting for the Browns, and he tried to lure me away from the Colts. It helped me get a pay raise. We talked about him moving to Baltimore around the time of the CFL team."

When the Browns moved to Baltimore, I was skeptical. For 12 years, I had been a "mercenary" NFL fan after the Colts left. I was "free" to follow any team I wanted and had chosen the New York Giants when I lived in New York City from 1985 through 1997.

During the first Ravens season in 1996, I saw footage of fans with birdcages on their heads and black beaks, and it all looked foreign to me. I hadn't lived in Baltimore since 1979 and didn't know who these people were or even who was on the team. I was slow to adapt because of what had been done to us in 1984 and what had happened to Cleveland.

As a poet, the only thing I liked about the Ravens was the connection to Edgar Allan Poe. I hadn't paid any attention at all to the Ravens until the Super Bowl run in 2000.

When I look back on it, the city of Baltimore and its fans became football mercenaries in 1996. We became as hardened as the players that are jettisoned to other teams after championship seasons. We grew desperate, believing that the only way we could get a team was to take one from another city. The Browns, Colts, Cardinals, Oilers, Raiders, and Rams all moved—giving us fair warning that we shouldn't get too attached to a team or its players. These franchise moves telegraphed what the NFL was becoming. The league didn't care about players and the community forming a bond. Moving the Browns to Baltimore was never about being fair—it was about money.

We received a savvy owner in Art Modell, who knew how to assemble the right talent to win—somebody whom the players loved and whose contributions to the modern-day NFL warranted a place in the Hall of Fame. He brought Ozzie Newsome with him, a former player who never missed a game in 13 years in the league. A Hall of Fame tight end, Ozzie was on his way to becoming one of the greatest general managers in the history of the game.

The Ravens won a Super Bowl in their first five years. It took the Indianapolis Colts 22 years, and the new Browns are still waiting. And all Modell wanted was a stadium.

Cleveland didn't acknowledge Art Modell's passing at its first home game in 2012, and the deceased former owner still maintained the position of public enemy No. 1, even outranking basketball player LeBron James, a homegrown talent who had left the Buckeye State for the Miami Heat in 2010. For Cleveland fans, Modell's death had served only to recycle old bile.

"The Cleveland fans hate the man. He's dead and they still hate him," said Bob Leetch, born and raised in Youngstown, Ohio, and a diehard Browns fan. "They rooted against the Ravens in the first Super Bowl. They root against them now. Everyone is still devastated that [Modell] moved the team."

It wasn't only the franchise move that angered Leetch, though that was the offense beyond the pale. He also still resents the ousting of Paul Brown. "He was one of the greatest coaches in the history of the NFL and was in the championship game every year for six years," said Leetch. "He drafted Jim Brown, the greatest running back of all time." Indeed, Coach Brown won an NCAA National Championship, four All-America Football Conference Championships, and three NFL Championships.

In 1961 Art Modell arrived in Cleveland with a group of investors from New York to buy majority ownership of the Browns, but he never got along with Paul Brown. Brown was a football genius, and Modell was a sales and marketing guy. When Modell received congratulations from Redskins owner George Preston Marshall about a trade that Paul Brown made without telling him involving Bobby Mitchell for Ernie Davis, Modell wasn't pleased and things went downhill from there.

The great Ohio football tradition is personified by Brown, an innovator and early promoter of racial integration in the NFL who revolutionized the game by introducing face masks, the scout team, the draw play, and the flanker position. He coached at Washington High School in Massillon, Ohio, a perennial powerhouse, and moved from there to Ohio State, where he was hired at the age of 36 to coach the Browns.

"I played for my St. Patrick's grade school on Sundays," said Leetch. "We'd have 20–30 teams out there, and the high school scouts were there filming games. If you were good, they'd offer your dad a job in Massillon so you could play football there."

Modell forced the revered Brown out in 1963, and Cleveland fans resented him from that point on despite winning an NFL championship in 1964, when the Browns beat the Baltimore Colts 27–0. According to David Halberstam in his Bill Belichick book, *The Education of a Coach,* Modell tried for 30 years to be a "major civic figure and philanthropist" and endear himself to the Cleveland public but was always derided as an outsider.

Modell's battles against public officials over a new stadium for football and his mounting debts in Cleveland trying to maintain Municipal Stadium led to his moving the Browns to Baltimore. He announced the move in November 1995. "I knew how much it meant to the fans. It was horrific," said Browns turned Ravens defensive end Rob Burnett. "Mr. Modell had put his life in jeopardy. Babe Ruth had hit a home run in Municipal Stadium. It was old. He did what he had to do."

Cleveland kept their colors and their name, but the team itself and two first-round draft picks that led to the 2000 Super Bowl win went to Baltimore. On November 7, 1995, Michael Olesker wrote a scathing piece in the *Baltimore Sun* on the Browns' move, imploring the NFL to name the team "The Baltimore Revenge."

"Baltimore Browns? Forget it. Browns is a name that obviously stands for nothing. Once, it stood for Jim Brown thundering across a line of scrimmage, and Otto Graham picking apart a secondary, and it stood for 70,000 half-frozen people filling up a rickety ballpark every Sunday, and no matter that icy wind whipping off Lake Erie because their football team, these Browns, these Kellys and Grozas and Motleys, they were theirs the way Baltimore once embraced its Colts, they belonged to the community that gave birth to them."

On December 17, 1995, the Browns played their last game in Municipal Stadium, a place so cavernous that 80,000 people turned up for the first Monday Night Football game in 1970, an epochal event that Art Modell had helped organize. In the fourth quarter against the Bengals, the fans ransacked the crumbling edifice with hacksaws and hammers to extract pieces of history.

On a damp Thursday night in Baltimore 17 years later, the Ravens and Browns played a scoreless first quarter in their first meeting of the 2012 season. Picking up where he left off from the Patriots game, Torrey Smith caught an 18-yard Joe Flacco touchdown pass to put the Ravens ahead 6–0. The extra point was no good. Smith would go on to catch six passes for 97 yards in the game.

Browns quarterback Brandon Weeden drove his team 94 yards for a late-second-quarter score, and the Ravens led 9–7 before the half. It had turned into another typical Ravens versus Browns scrum-laden deadlock. Typical of the hard hitting, Browns return specialist Josh Cribbs had to leave the game with a concussion after having his helmet knocked off and the ball punched loose by Ravens linebacker Dannell Ellerbe.

The NFL Network was broadcasting the Thursday night game in Baltimore and was set to release a few days later a documentary entitled *A Football Life: Cleveland 1995.* The documentary tells the story of a Cleveland franchise that was coming off an 11–5 season in 1994 with sights on a Super Bowl appearance. Head coach Bill Belichick had assembled a coaching staff that included nine future NFL head coaches and general managers and three major college head coaches: Ozzie Newsome, Scott Pioli, Mike Tannenbaum, Thomas Dimitroff, Jim Schwartz, Nick Saban, Kirk Ferentz, and Eric Mangini among them. "We wanted a tough, hard-nosed blue-collar football team. That's what Cleveland is, and that's what we wanted our team to be," said Belichick in the film.

When he arrived in Baltimore, Ozzie Newsome substituted "Baltimore" for "Cleveland" and finished building the team that Belichick had envisioned. They had some stray pieces in defensive end Rob Burnett, kicker Matt Stover, and special teams standout Bennie Thompson. The draft picks were already in place, and Newsome bypassed Modell's preference for the troubled running back Lawrence Phillips in order to pick Jonathan Ogden and, later in the round, Ray Lewis. "The Ray Lewis pick was pretty much done before the plane ever left to go to Baltimore," said

Mike Lombardi, who was Belichick's personnel assistant in Cleveland. With Ogden and Lewis, and a mixture of veterans like Shannon Sharpe, Rod Woodson, and Tony Siragusa, who joined the team in 1997, the Ravens won their first Super Bowl.

"When I won in 2000 [with the Ravens] I owe a lot of that to Belichick," said Newsome in the film.

But it had been a long 12 years since the 2000 Super Bowl season. For several years, the team struggled to score touchdowns and had no offense to speak of. It wasn't until the 2008 draft that the Ravens landed quarterback Joe Flacco and running back Ray Rice to help solidify the foundation of what they hoped would become a prolific offensive attack.

In 2010, they added another steely-eyed veteran, the breed that Newsome was known for finding, a tackle-breaking, stiff-arming wide receiver from the Arizona Cardinals looking to clutch a Lombardi Trophy named Anquan Boldin. In the second half against the Browns, Boldin took over.

The aggressive receiver snared three passes for 60 yards on the opening drive of the third quarter. On the last one, he snatched the ball in the right flat and stiff-armed and bulled his way to the 2-yard line. Flacco ran it in from there to put the Ravens ahead 16–7. Boldin would finish the game with nine catches and 131 yards.

On offense, the Browns had targeted cornerback Cary Williams all night, following the same strategy the Patriots' Tom Brady had exploited in the game four days before. Williams had spent the days since taking heat in the press for his failings, but redemption came late in the third quarter. Down 16–10, Browns quarterback Brandon Weeden tried to connect with Travis Benjamin, and Williams read it all the way, intercepting the pass and returning it 63 yards for a touchdown.

Still, the Browns refused to die. Twice they drove to the Ravens' 30 and kicked field goals to trail 23–16. With a minute left, they started from their own 10-yard line and again moved the ball into scoring position. With a first and 10 from the Ravens' 33, Weeden spiked the ball to stop the clock. On second down, safety Ed Reed came across the field to knock the ball away from Jordan Norwood at the last second in the end zone. On third down, Jimmy Smith did the same thing to receiver Greg Little. Jordan Cameron had the ball in his hands on fourth down, but Reed knocked it away again. A Paul Kruger penalty gave Weeden one more chance, and this time the ball sailed out of the end zone.

The Ravens secondary had denied a game-tying touchdown three times in a row and returned an interception for a score. The game had come down to the last play—a situation that suited the veteran-led 2012 Ravens.

"We're gonna have a lot of great-looking victories," said John Harbaugh in his postgame speech posted on the Ravens Web site. His voice rose in the locker room as he addressed his team. "We're going to have a lot of ass-kicking victories around here, and we're going to have some victories that look like this one right here. You gotta have both to go where we are going."

The defense wasn't built to shut teams down anymore. Ray Lewis, Terrell Suggs, and Ed Reed had accomplished that during the first decade of the twenty-first century. "In the early days, it was a race to the ball," said ex-Ravens defensive end Rob Burnett. "We were the clean-up crew." The 2012 defense had evolved into a unit that had weaknesses and holes, but was more savvy and nuanced. In a short field close to the goal line it was becoming more difficult for the opposition to solve. Approaching 40 years of combined experience in the NFL studying offenses, Lewis, Suggs, and Reed instinctively knew, more often than not, what the other team was going to try.

"Ray Lewis is always studying and evaluating. He's watching players in practice. He's grading himself every day," said Colts great Lenny Moore, who makes frequent visits to the training facility to watch practice. "He studies everything."

The 2012 season would depend on the Ravens' scoring more points than their opponents, because the defense would not be able to shut anyone down completely. The unit would make adjustments and get stronger during the course of games and would develop a talent for making big plays at the right time, but it needed a capable offense to back it up on the occasions it failed.

The defense began to rally around Lewis, Reed, and Suggs (after he returned from injury in Game 7) and sporadically played with their fury. Linebackers Kruger and Ellerbe had career years chasing down quarterbacks and running backs. Bernard Pollard delivered punishing hits at crucial times. Defensive linemen Haloti Ngata, Pernell McPhee, and Arthur Jones blocked passes and made sacks when games hung in the balance. Defensive backs Corey Graham, Cary Williams, and Chykie Brown seized victories with deflections and interceptions.

"It ain't about playing perfect," said Ray Lewis in the postgame locker room huddle. "It's about wins. Wins define championships. We learned that last week. We learned that last year with a loss that we could have played better. Now let's go dominate Kansas City."

But no game for the 2012 Ravens was going to be that easy. The Chiefs were 1–2 and coming off a loss at home to the Chargers. They were desperate to turn their season around against the Ravens. Reed would tell his team after the game was over that "you knew they were going to play their hearts out" because they had just been "smashed at home the week before."

The Chiefs' home, Arrowhead Stadium, is lodged in the subconscious of every true football fan. The crowd noise is deafening, and the Chiefs thrive on it. The place has a mystique. It's a football Mecca in the geographical middle of the country. Len Dawson, Buck Buchanan, and Curley Culp played on that field. Jan Stenerud kicked field goals. Joe Montana ended his career there. When the Chiefs line up to kick off in their sun-bleached white uniforms and cherry red helmets with ridged arrowhead logos, they resemble a warrior nation. The scene brings you back to the first AFL-NFL Super Bowl and Kansas City's dapper coach Hank Stram in a topcoat matching wits with Vince Lombardi. Though the Chiefs lost that game 35–10, they won Super Bowl IV after the 1969 season against the Vikings, proving that the Jets' triumph over the Colts the year before had been no fluke and that the AFL was the equal of the NFL.

As a boy, I had fabled KC quarterback Len Dawson's football card, and of all the uniforms in professional football, the Chiefs always took me back to my grade school readings about Crazy Horse, Chief Joseph of the Nez Perce, and Geronimo. I remember my father telling me stories about Chiefs defensive back Fred "The Hammer" Williamson and how "The Hammer" was going to knock out the Packer receivers in the Super Bowl. The Packers called a sweep, and Williamson took a knee to the head and broke his arm on the play.

In the Week 5 preparation for the Kansas City Chiefs, Ravens offensive coordinator Cam Cameron knew he would be facing a fierce defense. Linebackers Derrick Johnson, Justin Houston, Tamba Hali, and Jovan Belcher anchored their 3–4 scheme. "Their defense is the issue. When the game is tight, that defense feeds off that crowd. So obviously, it is going to be a big challenge for us," said Cameron.

Sure enough, the game started off as a defensive struggle. A Ray Rice 37-yard run late in the first quarter led to the first of three field goals in the game by Justin Tucker. Chiefs running back Jamaal Charles meanwhile slashed through the Ravens defense the entire first half, gaining 125 yards. Fortunately, his colleagues on offense didn't help out much, and his efforts only resulted in three points for Kansas City.

At halftime, the Ravens made defensive adjustments to set the edge and stop the Kansas City running game. In the second half, Charles gained only 15 yards. "We knew the ball wasn't going over heads. The game turned into our type of game," meaning a physical war, said Ray Lewis in a video posted on the Ravens Web site. He had ended his pregame talk with the cheer "Up front," meaning they would try to dominate the line of scrimmage. That didn't happen in the first 30 minutes, but it did in the second half.

Lewis sensed that the Chiefs were going to play a conservative game the rest of the way. They didn't have a quarterback in Matt

Cassel or in back-up Brady Quinn who had a strong enough arm to go deep or who could outsmart Ed Reed and the secondary and throw over the top of the defense. Chiefs head coach Romeo Crennel had faced Reed, Suggs, and Lewis many times during his days coaching the Cleveland Browns. While those three players had lost aspects of their athleticism, they had spent thousands of hours fine-tuning their football intellects. They had learned to anticipate what play was being called, and Crennel wasn't going to take a chance.

The biggest play of the game turned out to be a Chiefs' first and goal from the Ravens' 1-yard line at the start of the third quarter with the score still tied 3–3. Deonte Thompson, the Ravens' kick returner, had fumbled the second-half kickoff. Cary Williams was called for interference on receiver Dwayne Bowe, moving the ball to the 1-yard line. But Cassel fumbled the ball on a keeper. Reed had screamed to Lewis that the quarterback sneak was coming, and when the ball was sprung loose, Reed scooped it up and ran out of the end zone for 13 yards. A Chiefs touchdown in a game like this would have shifted the momentum and allowed the Kansas City defense to take pot shots against a flat Ravens offense. Instead, Reed and the defense had kept the game tied, and the Ravens eventually took a 9–3 lead on two field goals.

The Kansas City crowd was so upset by the Chiefs' offensive ineptitude that it cheered when Cassel got injured in the fourth quarter and Brady Quinn took over at quarterback. Quinn passed to Bowe for what looked like a go-ahead touchdown, but a penalty nullified the score, and the Chiefs settled for a field goal, leaving the Ravens ahead 9–6.

Then the Ravens got two big first downs, or most likely they would have been defending their goal line again. On a third and 15, Flacco left the pocket and scampered 16 yards. His running style for someone 6 feet 6 inches and 230 pounds is odd in that he takes very small steps, almost as though he is stepping quickly across hot coals. Rice got the next first down by the nose of the pigskin to cap off a 117-yard day on the ground, and the Ravens ran out the clock from there. "Last year, we lost games like this on the road," said safety Bernard Pollard in a locker room video posted on the Ravens Web site after the game. "Was it pretty? No. Is every game gonna be pretty, no."

On the Monday after the game, Harbaugh spoke to reporters. "There are a lot of things we are not pleased with," he said. "We did not have our best stuff. It was not a style point win. We move on and get ready for the Dallas Cowboys."

At one point during the conversation, Harbaugh became annoyed with a reporter who asked him why it took the offense so long to get in a rhythm and why they couldn't move the chains and get first downs earlier in the game. They had not converted a first down in the first quarter since Week 1 against the Bengals.

Harbaugh's smile turned serious, and his answer hinted at deeper issues with the Ravens offense. "There's a lot of reasons," he said, his countenance changing to express that a line had been crossed. "None that I am interested in sharing with you." It was clear that the performance of his offense had been wearing on him, and not just for the last three weeks but years.

Coach Harbaugh and his staff had work to do to contain the Dallas Cowboys pass rush and their talented wide receivers Dez Bryant, Miles Austin, and Jason Witten.

While an assistant, Cowboys coach Jason Garrett had been offered the Ravens coaching job ahead of John Harbaugh, but he had elected to stay in Dallas, eventually securing the head coaching slot there. I knew of Garrett and his father Jim from my graduate school days at Columbia University. During my first year in 1985, Jim coached the Columbia Lions—for whom the fabled Jack Kerouac briefly played running back—to a 0–10 season and extended what was then the nation's longest college football losing streak. He had scouted for Tom Landry and had played a few pro seasons, but that was his last in coaching. Jason and his two brothers moved on to Princeton after Jim was fired. Columbia ended up beating Princeton 16–13 on a rainy Saturday at Baker Field in 1988 to end the losing streak at 44 games.

The Dallas Cowboys took the field on October 14, 2012, having never beaten the Baltimore Ravens. Baltimore had even ruined the last game ever played in Texas Stadium with a 33–24 win in 2008 that included an 82-yard run from scrimmage by Ravens fullback Le'Ron McClain. Owner Jerry Jones replaced it in 2009 with a $1.3 billion stadium that seated 85,000.

The Cowboys were coming off a bye week and had started the season 2–2 after losing in Chicago to the Bears. They jumped out in front 10–3 on a Felix Jones touchdown run and a Dan Bailey field goal. The Ravens struck back, aided by a 43-yard screen to Ray Rice to tie the game at 10–10.

Early in the game, the Ravens suffered two catastrophic losses on defense. In the first quarter, Lardarius Webb collided with wide receiver Dez Bryant, and his knee buckled on the turf at M&T Bank Stadium—he'd torn his ACL and was lost for the season. Two plays before that, on the first play of the series, linebacker Ray Lewis got hurt making a tackle. He stayed on the field briefly, then was trying to leave when the Cowboys ran to the line and called a quick play. Running back Phillip Tanner ran right at Lewis and he made a one-arm tackle, his right limb dangling at his side. The press also described Lewis's injury as season ending, but he did not confirm that judgment.

The Ravens surged ahead just before half on three passes for 54 yards to Anquan Boldin, who was now making a name for himself in any Ravens game that was on the line. In the interstices of key drives, his name was always there. Torrey Smith finished the drive with an 18-yard touchdown catch. In the NFL Films highlights of the game it's clear John Harbaugh was overjoyed with his embattled offensive coordinator. "That's a helluva job Coach Cameron, wow," he said, patting him on the back.

It had been stunning. In a minute and 10 seconds the offense had marched 80 yards in eight plays. It was times like this that gave Coach Harbaugh hope that his long-time colleague and friend would overcome the constant criticism and finally deliver the consistent results that had eluded him in Baltimore. When he coached at Indiana, Cameron had made Harbaugh special teams coordinator in 1997, jump-starting a coaching career that at the time had gone stale. Harbaugh had wanted nothing more than to see "Coach Cam" succeed.

After Dallas kicked a field goal to cut the lead to 17–13, they kicked off to newly installed kickoff returner Jacoby Jones, who was handed the job after rookie returner Deonte Thompson had fumbled in Kansas City. Jones fielded the ball 8 yards deep in the end zone and started up through a seam on the right side of the field. A crushing block by Anthony Allen opened the hole, and Jones had only the kicker to beat. He raced 108 yards for a touchdown, breaking an NFL record. "I ran past my blocking," Jones told sportscaster Keith Mills, who had asked how he made the decision to return a ball that deep in the end zone. "When you get that itch, you want to scratch it. I scratched it. It's like red velvet cake over here and straight pound cake on the other."

The Ravens led 31–23 with four minutes left when Dallas quarterback Tony Romo took over. On fourth and 10 from the Ravens' 46, he completed a pass to Jason Witten. Again on fourth and 10, this time from the Ravens' 32, he completed a pass to Witten for 16 yards. On fourth and 1 from the Ravens' 4, he found receiver Dez Bryant for a touchdown, beating Ed Reed with 36 seconds left in the game. Dallas went for two points, throwing to Bryant again on the same play, and this time the Ravens stopped them to preserve their slim lead.

But the Cowboys were not finished. They recovered an onside kick and moved the ball to the Ravens' 34-yard line with 6 seconds left. Bailey's field goal attempt had plenty of distance but sailed wide, and the Ravens survived another last-second comeback attempt. Good teams enjoy good luck.

"We stepped up all three phases of the game when we had to," Harbaugh said in the locker room after the game. "That's what championship teams do."

Long-time Baltimore Ravens fan, writer, and filmmaker Charles Cohen was watching the season unfold, and a phrase now came to him that described what was happening with the 2012 team. Cohen designed and printed a thousand copies of a T-shirt reading, "Winning Ugly Is a Beautiful Thing."

The Ravens had perfected the art of unattractive victories and at times prided themselves on these types of wins. It was part of their heritage. *Sun* reporter Mike Preston had used the phrase "Winning Ugly" to describe their playing style as early as 2000. The Ravens defense spent most of its time back then completely silencing the offense of other teams.

For the most part, the Ravens didn't play shootouts and high-scoring games in the early days. The primary goal of the Ravens offense was to move the ball far enough for Matt Stover to kick field goals. There had been several prolonged touchdown droughts, including one that lasted five games in 2000, that prompted the message board comment "Quoth the Raven Neverscore." For the better part of a decade from 2000 to 2008, they had also racked up some ugly losses. But they had never been a "pretty" team to watch like New England, New Orleans, or Green Bay when they were winning.

Cohen's mantra stated the obvious. In 2012, Harbaugh still believed in "power football," and their playing style after 17 years was essentially the same. Cam Cameron added the no-huddle in 2012 to offer a different look, but Harbaugh hadn't strayed from the original blueprint—he just balanced it more, and so the defense no longer ruled the team. He finally had leaders on the other side of the ball in Joe Flacco and Ray Rice.

"We don't win games the way the NFL wants us to," Cohen told me over a sandwich at Tamber's where Colts tight end Jim Mutscheller used to take his wife. "We don't put a ton of points on the board. We are like the Steelers and the Giants. The Ravens are like Baltimore—ugly and cool at the same time. The whole place is a lovable mess. I mean, it doesn't get any uglier than *The Wire,* does it?" He was referring to David Simon's television show that revealed the inner workings of Baltimore's drug trade, corruption in city government, a struggling school system, and the decline of one of the nation's finest newspapers, the *Baltimore Sun.*

Mirroring the city, the Ravens were an acquired taste like the tangy mustard scraped with a forefinger from the carapace of a Maryland crab. There wasn't anything cute about them. They were the pit bull mixes of the NFL, lovable and messy.

Cohen's T-shirt was met with mixed reviews in the parking lots around the stadium. Some welcomed the homelier aspects of the team's playing style, and others eschewed it. But the Ravens had formed an identity for the 2012 season that was more than a thing of beauty. At 5–1, they were the best team in their division.

3. A Good Old-Fashioned Texas Ass Kicking

The possession of the pigskin is as charged
as one of the muses' arched crown of sonnets.
The line moving in tandem like a wave held
together and moving forward in its own delve. . . .
From outside the lines only the worshippers ogle
and fade away; never the glory.

—Scott Hightower

HOUSTON TEXAN Jacoby Jones prepared to receive a punt in the frigid Baltimore weather on his own 10-yard line. Leading 3–0 in the divisional round of the playoffs in Baltimore on January 15, 2012, the Texans were focused on increasing their lead on the road.

Ravens punter Sam Koch's ball bounced up off the turf, and Jones tried to catch it on the run with the Ravens pursuit on top of him. The ball hit him in the center of the shoulder pads just as Cary Williams made the tackle, and the ball squirted out into the hands of Ravens rookie defensive back Jimmy Smith, who carried it to the 2-yard line. Three plays later, the Ravens scored to take a 7–3 advantage. The play permanently swung the momentum of the game to the Ravens, and the muffed punt was the last mistake Jones would make as a Houston Texan.

In his Texans career Jones had dropped punts and passes, danced, wriggled, and at times looked like he was running in circles. Star Pizza's sign in Houston read, "Not even Jacoby Jones could fumble our pizza." Now Jones would be blamed for this bitter loss to the Ravens and would be released. As a result, the play also led to his becoming a major force in Baltimore's 2012 Super Bowl run.

This AFC Wildcard game—one that played out like many others in the Harbaugh era—helped shape the Ravens' 2012 Super Bowl season in other ways. The Ravens offense had done what it had to, and the defense had held on. This workmanlike approach had characterized their successes of the past three seasons—except when it fell short. The Houston playoff game came dangerously close to falling into another category, games the Ravens had under control and forgot to win.

The Texans came into the league as an expansion team in 2002. The 2011 postseason marked their first playoff appearance after years of lackluster teams that faltered when draft picks like quarterback David Carr didn't deliver. It had been a breakout year for Houston, which began winning with a strong defense and a dangerous offense assembled by general manager Rick Smith, head coach Gary Kubiak, and defensive coordinator Wade Phillips. The Texans had won 8 of their last 11 games and were not intimidated by Baltimore in the playoff game.

I watched that game at the top of the Ravens' stadium with my Aunt Carol, a former circuit court judge in Baltimore City and a long-time Colts fan who had switched over to the Ravens. An icy wind tore into the backs of our necks.

We shivered together in the back row against the fence. My father's sister and a former Sister of Mercy who defected around the time of my parents' divorce, Carol taught me how to run a post pattern, a square out, and a buttonhook. We talked about those days and laughed with the other characters in our section, people like Butch the pipefitter and Dave the facilities manager, good family men who knocked back a few beers and let loose a little in the stands on Sunday.

The Texans were without injured starting quarterback Matt Schaub. Backup T. J. Yates started for him, a tall job for a rookie who would be facing the vaunted Ravens defense and playing in front of a hostile crowd hungry for their first home playoff game in five years.

Houston had brought to Baltimore its own menacing defense, led by Connor Barwin and J. J. Watt, as well as an offense that featured one of the league's best running backs, Arian Foster, and All-Pro receiver Andre Johnson. The Texans stopped the Ravens on their opening drive, kicked a field goal on their first possession, and were about to get the ball back with a chance to extend their lead when Jones fumbled.

After the Jones miscue, the Ravens scored twice to lead 17–3. The Texans closed to within four points at half, 17–13, but two second-half interceptions allowed the Ravens to keep the Texans at arm's length despite a sputtering offense.

At halftime, my aunt told me she had a "friend" with a skybox. I had never been to one in the Ravens' stadium, so we scurried down the ramp to meet a messenger at the club level entrance. I asked who the friend was and my aunt said nothing.

Carol had put away dozens of hardened criminals—drug dealers and murderers—in a distinguished 30-year career as a Baltimore judge. She taught me about life in the city of Baltimore with certain sparingly used phrases like "today's witness is tomorrow's defendant."

We met her contact, a young woman who turned to my aunt and said, "Martin and Katie will be happy to see you." Politics had suddenly intervened. We were headed to the sky box of Maryland Governor Martin O'Malley.

Once inside, he shook my hand and told me that Carol had taught him "how to be a good assistant state's attorney." It took me by surprise and choked me up. The woman who bought me my first pair of shoulder pads had positively influenced the state's most visible public leader. It immediately became my single greatest moment at a professional football game.

O'Malley grew up in Bethesda organizing football games with his younger brothers and played for Gonzaga High in Washington, D.C. Now he and his father-in-law—former Maryland Attorney

General J. Joseph Curran, Jr.—watched the Ravens intently from stools at the window.

After exchanging pleasantries, I found a seat outside in the cold and got back to the game. Watching sports, particularly football, from a skybox had always pained me. A skybox is a dead zone, not quite your living room and certainly not the grandstands. I don't have time for the niceties and conversation and all the potential to miss the action. Watching football in the weather enhances the experience.

As the game grew tense on the field, the governor's box turned into a shelter from the cold for many. More and more people doubled up on chairs and sat around in a circle on the floor. The Ravens spent the entire second half keeping the Texans at arm's length but they could never quite finish them off. I longed for the upper deck—the football gods were punishing me.

It was Ravens football at its ugliest, a brawling and butt-ugly trench war. The Ravens were focused on defense, on exerting their will and making the Texans offense earn every yard. The purple and black did everything the NFL no longer wanted—bone-jarring, ball-separating hits on defense and at times a plodding ball-control style on offense. As a fan you knew they would be defending the goal line as time expired. They had trouble closing out games and embraced living dangerously as part of their nature. In this game they especially struggled in short-yardage situations.

Ed Reed, who had dropped two interceptions, appeared to seal the victory with less than two minutes remaining, falling back into the end zone with a spectacular interception. He caught the ball and then dangerously extended his arm to show the crowd and the referees that he had it before hitting the ground.

Ray Rice gained 9 yards on first down and was stopped for no gain on the next play. Vonta Leach was stopped on a third and 1 for no gain to force a punt that would give the ball back to Houston with time running out. The play illustrated a hallmark trait of the Cam Cameron–led Ravens offense. In short-yardage situations, he often called for a run up the middle. The defense knew it was coming, and the fans did too.

Knowing Rice, however, it could also have been his preference to ram the ball into the teeth of the defense. In his first day of training camp in 2008, Rice ran to the sidelines to avoid Ray Lewis, who was waiting for him in the middle of the field. Lewis told him never to do that again, and he didn't.

A date with the Patriots in the AFC Championship game came down to a T. J. Yates Hail Mary pass with 14 seconds left. The ball fell incomplete into the end zone amid a pile of Ravens defenders and Texans receivers. It was the first Ravens playoff victory at home since the 2000 Super Bowl season. "I always say there is a right way to do things, there is a wrong way to do things, and there is just the Ravens' way of doing things," linebacker Terrell Suggs was quoted in the *Baltimore Sun* after the game.

The Ravens were moving on to face the Patriots after a 20–13 win that had been closer than it needed to be. Their inability to finish off opponents in 2011 was evident against Houston and would play a role in the New England game as well.

Ed Reed called out his quarterback on the Monday before the AFC Championship. "I think Joe was kind of rattled a little bit by [Houston's] defense," Reed said on Sirius XM NFL Radio. The Texans, said Reed, "had a lot of guys in the box on him. And, I mean, they were getting to him. I think a couple times he needed to get rid of the ball. I don't know how much of the play-calling . . . but it just didn't look like he had a hold on the offense. It was just kind of like the coaching staff was telling him throw the ball or get it here, you know, get it to certain guys. And he can't play like that."

Reed had provided a glimpse into the tension that existed between Cam Cameron and Flacco. Joe had been sacked five times in the game, and Watt and Barwin wreaked havoc on the Ravens offensive line. They went three and out eight times in the game. Houston had shut down the passing lanes and the blocking schemes. During crucial times in games Cameron continued to see Joe as the 2008 rookie who was asked to just manage the game and control the time of possession.

The muffed punt that sealed Jacoby Jones's fate in Houston added a much-needed dimension to the Ravens' 2012 offense—a game changer with speed who could stretch the field. Jones would take the pressure off an offense that lacked consistency and an identity.

The Houston playoff game gave the Ravens a gift that vastly improved their offense in 2012. If Jones had managed to field that punt, he might still be a Texan and the Ravens would be a team with one or two more losses in a season that might not have ended at the Super Bowl. As for Jones's reaction to signing with Baltimore, "As soon as I saw [a] Maryland [area code] pop up on my phone, I was thinking about a Super Bowl ring. I was ready to roll."

The Houston Texans couldn't wait for the Baltimore Ravens to arrive in their city on October 21, 2012. They were eager to atone for that playoff loss and not only defeated the Ravens, but embarrassed and physically dismantled them. It is not often that the Ravens take a beating like this one. Their motto, "Play like a Raven," means, among other things, play tough physical football.

In the long run, the 43–13 loss helped strengthen the Ravens and brought them closer together at a critical juncture. Houston had helped the Ravens improve their roster: along with Jacoby Jones, Baltimore now had former Texans safety Bernard Pollard and fullback Vonta Leach. Now by delivering a punishing defeat, Houston provided a catalyst for the Ravens' pursuit of a second Lombardi Trophy.

Starting out 5–1 to begin the season, the Ravens met the Texans in Houston without two key defensive starters. In the previous week's game against the Dallas Cowboys, the Ravens had lost cornerback Lardarius Webb and linebacker Ray Lewis, and they both would likely be out for the remainder of the regular season despite Lewis's promise that he would be back.

These injuries cast serious doubts on the Ravens' Super Bowl aspirations. But there was also room for hope. Coming back from an Achilles tendon injury, Terrell Suggs had talked about being ready for the Houston game. He had started practicing with the team on October 18. Whenever he appeared on the sidelines at home games and the camera showed him on the big screen, he would hold up seven fingers—meaning he would return in Week 7. His immediate family and relatives had purchased tickets to the game. Suggs's absence had led to a Ravens defense that was being gashed for an average of 296 yards per game. When the Ravens came through the tunnel in Houston, number 55 was there. He had returned to the team in record time. Sports radio talk show host Glenn Younes said, "The idea of a five-month two-week comeback is insane, but in the world of a dude that's more freak than normal I guess it's as sane as he is."

Terrell Suggs stands 6 feet 3 inches and weighs 260 pounds. He once ran for 367 yards as a running back for his high school football team. He lettered three times in basketball in high school and plays the outside linebacker position with the agility of a power forward. He is, according to Patriots Pro Bowl guard Logan Mankins, a "freak of an athlete" and can run over you. Mankins believes that Suggs is in an elite class of players who are stronger and faster than the rest.

"If you could get the Madden game and design your own player," said Bengals offensive tackle Andrew Whitworth on the Ravens Web site, "it would be hard to design anyone that wouldn't look like 'T-Suggs.' He's got it all: He's ripped up, he's big, he's fast, he's strong, he is intimidating looking. I'd create him eleven times over. He's one of those ultimate talents." On the field and on the sidelines, he has a running dialogue with players and fans. "American Express," he shouts after Dennis Pitta makes a reception for the Ravens. "He's everywhere you want to be."

It was a clear fall day in Houston but the Texans elected to play the game with the roof closed. Ravens columnist John Eisenberg posted on the Ravens Web site that the Texans wanted it to be loud in the stadium to disrupt the Ravens hurry-up offense. "Oh, the roof will be closed. There's no question," a Houston-based reporter had told him. "Because the Ravens run a no-huddle offense. The Texans want it to be loud in here today."

The week before, Houston had lost its first game of the season in embarrassing fashion to the Green Bay Packers 42–24 at home. Combined with the Texans' continued bitterness over the playoff loss to Baltimore the previous year, this gave Houston multiple reasons for revenge. It was "Battle Red" day in Houston, and the fans and the players wore red jerseys reserved for a couple of important games a year. The Houston defense likes it "because it keeps the blood flowing."

This is a football team in a town of rodeo worshippers. The Texans are not America's team like the Cowboys once claimed to be—a team whose image tracks more to the gentility of the Lone Star State. Jerry Jones resembles a football version of Jock Ewing presiding over martinis uptown at the Melrose Hotel with the frosted hair and gold lamé gown set.

These Houston Texans don't track back to the Texicans of San Antonio de Béxar and Davy Crockett. They are the wildcatters of big oil with their Teutonic longhorn logo in the colors of "deep steel blue," "battle red," and "liberty white."

"The Texans have always [played] second fiddle to the Cowboys," said Oilers-turned-Texans fan Tim Fuller. "But now the tide has turned and we have the better team. We still haven't won the big one yet."

Fuller remembered feeling the stands in the Astrodome shaking when 70,000 fans greeted the Oilers after an AFC Championship loss to the Steelers in 1978. The city had sustained a heartbreaking loss after the Oilers left in 1996. Their former head coach Bum Phillips, the cattle rancher, had returned to help Gary Kubiak and the city of Houston finally win the big one and get to a Super Bowl. The fans couldn't wait to see the Ravens dismembered by their gigantic defensive line.

The Ravens no-huddle offense was effective on their first drive, moving the ball to the Texans' 38-yard line. But listening to Gerry

Sandusky call the game on the radio while coaching my daughter's soccer team, I knew when the Ravens didn't score a touchdown that it was going to be a long day. Justin Tucker kicked a 51-yard field goal to give the Ravens a deceptive early lead, 3–0.

On Houston's next possession, Suggs looked every bit like the 2011 Defensive Player of the Year he had been, sacking Matt Schaub for an 8-yard loss. It was the last highlight of the day for the Ravens.

Returning the favor, Connor Barwin sacked Joe Flacco for a safety on the next possession, and the scoreboard read like a baseball score at 3–2. The Ravens punted to the Texans. Schaub moved the ball into Ravens territory and hit Kevin Walters on a 25-yard touchdown strike to make it 9–3.

The Texans came for Flacco on the next series, and a pass intended for Torrey Smith was tipped by J. J. Watt and wound up in the hands of Jonathan Joseph, who raced 52 yards for a touchdown. Houston batted balls and collapsed the Ravens line like the adobe walls of the Alamo mission, putting extreme pressure on Flacco all day. The Texans led at the half, 29–3. "I told Flacco, 'It's impressive you're still in the game,'" said Barwin in the *Houston Chronicle.* "I hit the [expletive] out of him a couple of times."

The Texans destroyed the Ravens, 43–13, and spoiled Suggs's return. They produced 476 yards of total offense. Arian Foster rushed for 98 yards. Andre Johnson caught eight balls for 89 yards in a good old-fashioned Texas ass kicking. Matt Schaub turned in a solid performance, throwing for 256 yards and two touchdowns.

"Poor Flacco had a quarterback rating of 45.4, which is like scoring an F-minus on an exam, with 147 yards passing and two interceptions," wrote Randy Harvey on a *Houston Chronicle* blog. "He also was sacked four times, was hurried eight times and had five passes deflected."

The lopsided loss, the worst of John Harbaugh's tenure, accentuated the problems facing the Ravens. The defense had again been ripped apart. This time they were not holding the opponent to field goals. Flacco and the no-huddle didn't fool the Houston defense, and they batted away many of his passes.

CBS Baltimore talk show host Glenn Younes excoriated the coaching staff on the radio as I drove my son Quinn to his football practice on Monday, October 22. "I know they are not intentionally trying to do a bad job," he said. "But how can you explain continually running a no-huddle and putting a defense on the field whose best player is recovering from an injury and the rest of the unit has been torched all season?"

The fan message boards called for Cam Cameron's head after the Houston game. Out of ten possessions in the game, only one lasted longer than two minutes. Ray Rice was a forgotten man. He had six carries and averaged 5.8 yards per carry, but his number was rarely called. In a thread entitled, "Seriously, Fire Cam Cameron Now," a fan wrote: "I'm 100% sick of him being the coordinator. 100% sick of it. This offense looks unprepared and out of rhythm all the time and succeeds in spite of poor coaching with its talent. I usually stand up for Harbaugh, but he's on my s*** list now until he gets rid of Cameron." The Ravens were now 5–2 at a point in the season when the AFC had only two winning teams.

Inside the locker room, John Harbaugh was worried. His team had just faltered in all aspects of the game. "I'm concerned about everything," Harbaugh said in his postgame comments to the *Baltimore Sun*. "You can talk about pretty much everything today. What aren't you concerned about? Sometimes you get tossed out of the bar. We came in with hype, with good intentions, and ready to do battle. I thought our guys fought. We kept running back in and they kept throwing us back out. . . . We'll have to regroup and play a lot better in the future."

One aspect of the Texans game provided a bright spot for the Ravens. Following up on his first kickoff return of the year for a touchdown against the Cowboys the week before, Jacoby Jones had returned six kickoffs for 196 yards against his old team. He ran one back 45 yards and another 41. He was fitting in as though he'd been with Baltimore his entire career.

After the Texans' thrashing, the players took their bye-week break while Ray Lewis remained in Miami, rehabbing his injured right arm. When the team gathered in the auditorium at their training facility, "The Castle," one week later on Halloween, John Harbaugh announced that they would be practicing that day in full pads—something that didn't happen in the middle of an NFL season.

The players erupted. Ed Reed and Bernard Pollard confronted their coach and expressed their frustration. Some players were still nursing nagging injuries and groaned at the thought of putting on pads. The discussion came close to veering out of control. "Coach Harbaugh opened up the floor, he asked us our opinion on things that were going good and things that wasn't going good and things that we needed to change. . . . And so I spoke up, Ed spoke up," said Pollard to Houston radio station KILT-AM after the season.

The discussion morphed into a group therapy session. The players leveled criticism at the plays being called and at Harbaugh's behavior. He was moody at times, distracted. The air cleared, the team began the practice session without pads. "I wasn't threatened by it," Harbaugh told NFL.com. "You know, they had some good points, and I had some good points. Other guys stood up and said some great things. To me, it embodied everything that you should have on a team."

It also embodied the Ravens' playing style. There were moments that had been difficult and "ugly" and others when the team came together. This time around, without Ray Lewis as a spokesperson and buffer, they were building trust. Nonetheless, in jerseys and shorts, they had a bad practice. The effort was lacking. They were going through the motions, dropping balls.

Kevin Van Valkenburg reported on ESPN that Reed then called out his teammates and told them that the trust they had just built with Coach Harbaugh in the "clearing the air" discussion had evaporated. Harbaugh had been brilliant in exercising restraint and letting the players have their say. He showed his team a side of his personality that was vulnerable but also confident in his abilities. The players left the meeting feeling that their voices had been heard and that Harbaugh had been a great sounding board.

John Harbaugh's leadership skills extended far beyond mediating an uprising. He was the son of a coach in what had to be one of the most competitive football families in America. His brother Jim was a fighter and so was he. They played peewee football in Toledo and Ann Arbor, where their father coached at the college level, and they would both become part of the great football tradition in Ohio and Michigan. John played at Miami of Ohio and Jim at Michigan. John had observed the dynamics of team interaction all his life. The Ravens' "mutiny" was easy to handle.

The "uprising" had been leaked to the media, and it was all over the newspapers and sports talk shows as a cathartic event—a "Kumbaya" moment when the Ravens all came together as a team. The Ravens front office let it play out that way. It had the Hollywood spin they wanted, and it took on a life of its own.

CBS Baltimore radio talk show host Steve Davis had a different take on the "mutiny" after the season. He said, "It was being portrayed as a 'come to Jesus moment,' but I don't think we will ever know for sure what went on in that room. I don't think it was the turning point. They continued to play badly after it happened. And now Ed Reed and Bernard Pollard are gone. I think the spin was convenient at the time, but it was more complex than that."

Ed Reed had defended his coach after the team's bad practice on Halloween, but they hadn't always gotten along over the years. Reed and Pollard had been the enforcers in the Ravens secondary, and the referees kept a watchful eye on them. Reed and Pollard had both been critical of the new NFL rules designed to reduce brain injuries and had been flagged all season for helmet-to-helmet hits.

Despite the penalties, they were both having great seasons and a positive effect on the younger defensive backs, but their status, like everyone else's, would be evaluated after the season was over. "If you ask me a question, I'm going to give you an honest answer," a bitter Bernard Pollard told Steve Davis in an interview after the season was over and he and Ed Reed were no longer Ravens. "Whoever leaked that [mutiny] story to the press should be ashamed of themselves."

John Harbaugh had listened to his players, and the Ravens had left that meeting feeling better about themselves and the team they were playing for. Harbaugh had sacrificed a small amount of his power to gain control of the locker room for the future.

One other significant change had come out of the wreckage of the Houston game. There was no more mention of the no-huddle offense.

The Browns now awaited the Ravens in Cleveland, where they always played Baltimore tough and the fans' hatred was as piercing as the arctic air off Lake Erie. Browns rooters demanded a good showing against the city that had stolen their team. Cleveland had won two out of its last three games, beating the Chargers and the Bengals. This one had all the makings of a defensive battle.

Buoyed by the Texans' thrashing of the Ravens, Cleveland fans sensed an upset in the making. They had an exciting rookie running back from Alabama in Trent Richardson. They had a solid rookie quarterback in Brandon Weeden from Oklahoma State and a good wide receiver named Travis Benjamin.

"Go ahead, temper your enthusiasm, Browns fans, that's what always happens," wrote Jimmy Weinland in the *Dawg Pound Daily*. "But make no mistake, this is the best chance the Browns have had to beat the Baltimore Ravens in four years. Everyone feels it. This is it. There is hope." Weinland pointed to Flacco's average road numbers and the absence of Webb and Lewis.

Unveiling an old school, two-pronged running attack featuring Ray Rice and rookie Bernard Pierce, the Ravens scored touchdowns on their first two possessions to take a 14–0 lead. Rice ran for 33 of his 98 yards on the first series including an 8-yard touchdown run. Pierce followed with a 12-yard touchdown run on the very next drive. Suddenly, the Ravens resembled the

Jamal Lewis teams of the early 2000s in churning up yards on the ground and running the clock.

On the next six possessions the Ravens punted, the offense going as stale as egg salad left out in the sun. Cleveland began chipping away at the Ravens lead on the toe of Phil Dawson. The Ravens held on to a tenuous 14–12 advantage in the second half when Brandon Weeden found Josh Gordon for a touchdown to put the Browns in front. But Cleveland was called for an illegal formation, and the play came back.

New Browns owner Jimmy Haslam threw his head back and covered his forehead. Still, his team did briefly take the lead on Dawson's fifth field goal of the day, 15–14. But Joe Flacco drove the Ravens down the field. He found Anquan Boldin for 21 yards. Ray Rice rumbled for 10 yards each on back-to-back plays, and Flacco hit Torrey Smith on a curl-in route. Smith did the rest, sprinting 19 yards for a touchdown. The Ravens went for a 2-point conversion and got it on another pass from Flacco to Boldin to stretch the lead to 7 points, 22–15.

The Ravens added another field goal after Cleveland went for it on fourth and 2 from their own 28 with just under four minutes left and lost the ball on downs. Then Ed Reed intercepted Weeden on a deep pass to Travis Benjamin. Cary Williams also had an interception. The Ravens secondary played a great game, kept the rookie quarterback confused, and eventually got inside his head.

The locker room "mutiny" had propelled the secondary to perform better. It was evident that Reed was molding ball hawks in his own image. He regularly held court at his home, watching tape with players, according to Kevin Van Valkenburg's ESPN article "Ed Reed, Hiding in Plain Sight." Reed would sit with a remote control and a pencil in his favorite seat, with Corey Graham, Chykie Brown, Cary Williams, and anyone else who wanted to talk football. He was teaching the game. No hellfire and brimstone from Reed.

He preached the routes, the coverage, and the responsibilities. The closeness of that unit helped the Ravens prevail in Cleveland.

A number of Weeden's balls landed in dead space with no receivers even close. When asked about Reed, Ravens columnist John Eisenberg said, "Reed has anchored the back of the defense for a decade, won games single-handedly. His contributions to the franchise are greater than almost anyone's."

The Browns stayed true to their losing ways. They had played well but had beaten themselves. Every year I drive to Chicago to visit my mother and stop outside of Cleveland. When I do, I think about the Browns teams of the mid to late 1980s. Without the Colts, I followed the Bernie Kosar teams and prayed they would beat quarterback John Elway and Denver just once in an AFC Championship. I didn't want Elway to win a Super Bowl after spurning Baltimore in the 1983 draft. He had refused to join the Colts and even threatened to pursue a baseball career with the New York Yankees, another team I disliked.

But "The Drive" changed my perception of him. In the 1987 AFC Championship game against the Browns, Elway had driven his team 98 yards in 15 plays to tie the score at 20 with 37 seconds remaining. The Broncos won in overtime, 23–20.

Not many athletes could drive a team 98 yards with a bitter wind in their faces and the game on the line. I respected Elway as a football player from that moment on. He was big shouldered, had a strong arm, and could take off with the ball and run people over. He was exciting to watch.

Kosar bore a likeness to my own Uncle Bernie, who took me to the Colts-Raiders playoff game in 1977. Bernie Bartoli had played halfback for the Parkville traveling team when he was young and flag football with Colt safety Bruce Laird and other Colts in his later years. Kosar, the former Miami Hurricane quarterback, was playing on knees that were like popsicle sticks by the end of his NFL career. His final touchdown pass to Michael Jackson had been drawn up in the dirt, and it had been the final straw for Bill Belichick. I had been in a huddle like that on the sandlot with a sniffling quarterback drawing routes on his frozen palm.

After an 11–5 season in 1994 and the Browns' move to Baltimore in 1995, Coach Belichick was fired and rejoined Bill Parcells in New England. Years later, he expressed regret at the way he handled the Kosar situation.

I drove out in 2007, the year a Phil Dawson field goal in OT for Cleveland beat the Ravens, 33–30. Coach Romeo Crennel's team finished 10–6 and things were looking up. Briefly, Cleveland was abuzz about the Browns. But it has been a long painful journey since the latter-day Ravens deserted the city, and the expansion Browns have struggled miserably. For followers of the Cleveland Browns, the wounds go far deeper than the diminishing specter of Robert Irsay in Baltimore. "No matter how efficiently [Baltimore] builds their team and runs their business they will always be the city that stole our team," wrote Craig Lyndall on the "Waiting for Next Year" blog in Cleveland before the game. "They will always be the people who used Art Modell without a care in the world for breaking our souls. They will seemingly never understand how hypocritical it is to despise the Irsay family and put Art Modell on a pedestal."

In 2000, Browns fans believed that Baltimore stole their Super Bowl—that Ray Lewis and Jonathan Ogden were *their* draft picks. John Harbaugh grew up following the Browns. He identified with them and said some nice things about the Browns after the game. "They are physical, they're tough, they're disciplined; they've got all the tools. They're young and they are building something here," he told CBS Cleveland.

Harbaugh deserves credit for achieving the right tone in the aftermath of a game that could have gone either way. He knew that the Ravens would not beat the Browns in every game during his coaching tenure with the Ravens. He's a Midwest guy, and his lineage and connection to the Browns appealed to Ozzie Newsome and Kevin Byrne when they interviewed him. Harbaugh was one of them.

Now the Ravens' record stood at 6–2. The Browns were not yet good enough to beat them. Joe Flacco had extended his record to 10 straight wins against Cleveland—an NFL record for a quarterback against one team.

On Sunday, November 11, the Oakland Raiders came to Baltimore. The 2012 Raiders were as hapless as the Browns, and the Ravens were fortunate to face these two teams after the bye week. The temporary lull in the intensity of the schedule would soon be ending.

The Raiders had finished with an 8–8 record in 2011 but were a dismal 3–6 so far in 2012. The mystique of the Raiders' "commitment to excellence" under Al Davis had vanished. The days when John Madden was a shrewd young coach of the crafty Fred Biletnikoff, who smeared his arms with a sticky mango-colored paste so he could catch touchdown passes from Ken Stabler, were long gone. The Raiders last chance at glory had come a decade ago when they were blown out by the Tampa Bay Buccaneers 48–21 in the 2002 Super Bowl. In 2001, in a playoff game against the Patriots on a snowy night in Foxborough, they were robbed when a Tom Brady fumble was overturned and became an incomplete pass, the infamous "tuck rule" incident.

The game between the Ravens and the Raiders resembled an intrasquad scrimmage or a preseason game. When Carson Palmer stumbled backward and fell down after a snap on their first drive, you sensed it would be a long day for the silver and black.

Sam Koch, the Ravens punter, scored his first ever touchdown on a fake field goal, and the Ravens offense exploded for a franchise-record 55 points. With the score 48–20, Ravens kick-return specialist Jacoby Jones stood deep in his own end zone to receive the kickoff. The deeper the kick, the more likely Jones would run it out. Jones caught the ball and came up through the middle of the field. He took a slight turn right and was gone—105 yards for the score. It was his second kickoff return for a touchdown in four weeks.

Jones had settled into his new team nicely, and they accepted him for who he was—someone with a wicked sense of humor who liked to break out in dance routines. It was a loose locker room in Baltimore. You had your preacher in Ray Lewis. There were the football geeks like Ed Reed with his playbook and pencil. Flacco and Pitta shared an old school bond like Johnny Unitas and Raymond Berry. Anquan Boldin—or "Q"—was a silent warrior boiling over with intensity. Kicker Justin Tucker, punter Sam Koch, and long snapper Morgan Cox called themselves the Wolfpack for reasons known only to them. And there was the outspoken Brendan Ayanbadejo, who liked to mix it up with the media on issues such as gay marriage. Ray Rice with his infectious prankster smile kept things light and played a comedian's role. Suggs, or "Sizzle" as he liked to call himself, a self-professed graduate of the fictitious "Ball So Hard" University that he founded in 2009 as an alternative to the school of hard knocks, served as mayor of the Ravens' ongoing freak show. "Ball So Hard" football tournaments are held in T-Sizzle's honor for Baltimore youth in the fall. The 2012 Ravens were a wicked and ripe concoction of personalities who left it all—the good, the bad, and most definitely the ugly—on the field.

Jacoby Jones had come home. With the Ravens, he could be himself and one day pursue his dream of showing the world his dance moves on the television show *Dancing with the Stars.*

"On this team, with so many different personalities, we just accept people for who they are," said Terrell Suggs on ProFootballTalk.com. "Our biggest thing in the locker room is to have fun and stay loose."

Part of the problem in Houston was that the coaches had never been sure of Jones's role. He was never the primary kick returner for the Texans. From 2007 through 2011, he had only returned 17 kicks. But he would go on to score seven touchdowns for the Ravens during the 2012 season. He returned three kicks and a punt for touchdowns and caught three touchdown passes—as well as two in the playoffs that will be immortalized by generations of Baltimore football fans to come. He would set a Super Bowl record in total yardage and rip off a 108-yard kickoff return—the longest ever in the 47-year history of the game.

The Ravens were 7–2 as they headed into Steeler week and a trip to Heinz Field. The crushing defeat in Houston had helped to clear the air, but lingering issues with the offense remained despite a 55-point explosion against a bad team. The Raiders were still adjusting to East Coast time when the game ended. As for Jacoby Jones, he was just warming up.

4. Fourth and 29

Hey diddle, diddle, Ray Rice up the middle.

—Ray Rice

THE RAVENS entered Week 11 of the 2012 NFL season with a 7–2 record. In nine games, they had won convincingly only twice, against Cincinnati and Oakland. They were vulnerable on defense without Ray Lewis and ineffective for long stretches on offense, especially on the road. The defense was ranked 27th in the NFL, but their red zone defense was ranked number one. Their red zone offense was ranked fifth overall—a good sign.

Preparing for their tenth game, they held a one-game lead over the Steelers atop the AFC North Division. The most difficult part of their schedule was upon them. They would face Pittsburgh twice in three weeks, a Chargers team that had beaten them the year before, a rejuvenated Redskins outfit suddenly vying for a playoff berth, and the Broncos with Peyton Manning behind center. The following week Peyton's brother Eli Manning and the 2011 Super Bowl Champion New York Giants would be in Baltimore. Beyond that, the season would end in Cincinnati against a surging Bengals team.

The Ravens met their most despised foe at Heinz Field in Pittsburgh for a Sunday night showdown on November 18, 2012. Steelers quarterback Ben Roethlisberger had injured his ribs and shoulder in a Monday night overtime win against the Kansas City Chiefs the week before and was not scheduled to play against the Ravens. Or so the Steelers camp was saying; in the past one learned not to believe those reports. Big Ben had experienced sore shoulders and ankles before; he had been hobbled and bloodied only to limp in and pull out a victory. Before Roethlisberger's injury, the Steelers had won four straight and were beginning to show a newly discovered source of speed on offense with receivers Emmanuel Sanders, Mike Wallace, and Antonio Brown.

They had a new fullback, Jonathan Dwyer, reminiscent of the "The Bus" from the 2006 Super Bowl champions, Jerome Bettis. Roethlisberger had begun to find his way around Todd Haley's new offensive schemes, and I worried that Pittsburgh was beginning to assemble the necessary pieces for another Super Bowl run.

Pittsburgh's defense, anchored by James Harrison, Troy Polamalu, and LaMarr Woodley, ranked number one in the NFL. After a 1–2 start, they had beaten the Redskins at home and the Giants in New York. They were 6–3 with a chance to tie Baltimore for the division lead.

Against the Ravens, the Steelers wore black and yellow horizontally striped uniforms from the 1934 team and started the veteran quarterback Byron Leftwich, a journeyman quarterback from Marshall who had played in just two games since 2009. Their jerseys were more suited for a team whose nickname was the yellow jackets and made them look like a work release crew on break from picking up trash on the Pennsylvania Turnpike. The Steelers reserved throwback uniforms for special occasions like the Ravens game every year, part of an effort to flaunt their 80-year tradition in the face of the fledgling 17-year-old franchise. But this time they looked more comical than fierce.

For more than a decade this has been one of the NFL's best and most heated rivalries. Before the game, Steelers nose tackle

Casey Hampton added this perspective in the *Pittsburgh Post-Gazette.* "You know 'hate' is a terrible word to say. I think they hate us, though. . . . Probably because we knock them out of the playoffs every year." The venom had tapered off in recent years, following receiver Hines Ward's retirement, but there had been trash talk, targeted hits, and near fisticuffs on the field.

Ward had leveled Ed Reed with a blindside block on a Monday Night Football game in 2007, prompting Reed to label him a "dirty player." Their feud went on for years and climaxed on Pittsburgh's first play from scrimmage in the 2010 playoffs, when they wrestled each other to the ground. Both teams shared a visceral hatred for each other, but they had also developed a mutual respect over the years. The game plans were conservative and did not include trickery or deception. Both teams were going to force their strengths on the other. The defense on both sides dominated the games, and usually the outcome came down to a mistake.

Late in the 2011 game in Pittsburgh, a penalty had moved the Steelers out of field goal range, and they punted to the Ravens, who scored the winning touchdown. Earlier in his career Joe Flacco had fumbled and thrown interceptions at crucial times, giving the Steelers key playoff and regular season victories.

The rivalry traveled with the Browns to Baltimore in 1996. The two teams knew each other intimately before the move and had hated each other for decades, going back to 1950 when the series began. The animosity was enhanced when the Browns became the Ravens.

Baltimore football fans remembered humiliating losses to the Steelers in 1975 and 1976—including a 40–14 massacre in Memorial Stadium. Steelers fans had sprung up in Baltimore during the 12-year aftermath of the Colts' departure. In the western parts of Maryland there was an affinity with the Steelers and a large community of fans. The old guard from Baltimore's Irish community respected the Rooney family, who owned the Steelers, and remembered that Art Rooney had supported the move of the Dallas Texans franchise to Baltimore in 1953 while Redskins owner George Preston Marshall did not because the team was encroaching on his market. I remember my grandfather Newton Smith tippling a shot of Imperial whiskey for the Rooneys when they won their first Super Bowl in 1975. We had just finished bowls of Queenie's Irish stew.

Before the 2012 game, Hines Ward gave an example of the rivalry's vitriolic nature. "One moment that stands out was when our bus pulled up to their stadium and there were three generations of a family there waiting for us. There was the grandfather, his son, and a little boy about 4. All three of 'em were giving us the finger. I just thought, 'Man, that's what the Steelers-Ravens game is all about.'"

From 1996 through 2010 the Steelers won 19 and lost 11 in the series, but in recent years the power has shifted slightly to the Ravens, who have taken 4 out of the last 7. The Ravens won both games in 2011, including a major turning point in Flacco's career in Week 9 of the 2011 season.

Fans in Baltimore were divided over their quarterback. His detractors remained skeptical of his abilities and wanted to see him develop more consistency. Facing Ben Roethlisberger in a prime-time showdown on a Sunday night, Flacco played one of the best games of his career and overcame his mistakes to produce a major victory and the second defeat of the Steelers and Roethlisberger in the same season—always a major accomplishment and popular with the fans.

The first half included a volley of field goals. The teams were evenly matched, with each trying to assert its will on the other. The Ravens held a tenuous 9–6 lead at halftime. A Terrell Suggs interception ended a Pittsburgh drive at the Ravens' 20-yard line to begin the second half.

Thirteen plays later, Ray Rice scored from 4 yards out to give the Ravens a 16–6 lead. By the end of the third quarter, the Steelers responded with a scoring drive that included a 30-yard pass from Roethlisberger to Heath Miller to close the gap to 16–13.

With the Ravens driving on the Pittsburgh 39 and the game under control, Flacco dropped back to pass and James Harrison sacked him, causing a fumble. Pittsburgh marched down the field and capped off the drive with a 29-yard touchdown pass to Mike Wallace after a Roethlisberger scramble. It looked like the same old story against the Steelers—another late-game collapse. "It was ear-piercing bedlam in there. The Steelers fans smelled victory after Flacco faltered as he'd done before against them," said Rob Duckwall of Baltimore, who had made the road trip to the Iron City.

With 2:24 remaining in the game, Flacco took over from his own 8-yard line. Pittsburgh fans around Duckwall recalled a late Flacco touchdown pass to ex-Raven receiver T. J. Houshmandzadeh in 2010, but that was a game Roethlisberger, who has been to the Super Bowl three times, had missed. Big Ben had a record of 7–3 against the Ravens at that time, as well as 2–0 in the playoffs. Any Ravens wins with him out of the lineup didn't really count to Steelers fans.

On second and eight from the Pittsburgh 37-yard line, Flacco went to Torrey Smith deep, and the pass was incomplete. On third down, he found Anquan Boldin for a first down to keep the drive alive. The Steelers called time out.

With 14 seconds to go, Flacco channeled Johnny Unitas—here in the Hall of Famer's hometown—as he again went with the rookie Smith, who gained separation from William Gay as he crossed the goal line and made the catch for the touchdown. The frenzied din of Heinz Field went silent. "That night, I felt something different," linebacker Ray Lewis told ESPN. "We will not lose this game. The team that never dies, that is who the Ravens are becoming."

Now in 2012 the Ravens had the opportunity to beat their nemesis for a third straight time, a feat they hadn't accomplished since the 2005–2006 season. It was a critical game for the Ravens to win because it would give them control of the division with a two-game lead.

In a shrewd and unexpected maneuver in their first meeting of the 2012 season—on a night when the Steelers were celebrating their 80th anniversary with Lynn Swann, L. C. Greenwood, Mean Joe Greene, John Stallworth, and Hines Ward in attendance—the Steelers went for it all on the first play of the game. They decided to test cornerback Cary Williams on a bomb to speedster Mike Wallace, and a penalty was called on the Ravens cornerback—though to me it looked like he had made a decent play on the ball. Pittsburgh had the ball on the Ravens' 37.

Leftwich ran 31 yards for a touchdown two plays later. He stumbled and fell as he crossed the goal line and injured his shoulder as he hit the ground, hampering his ability to throw for the rest of the game. The Steelers led 7–0.

After the ball changed hands again, the Ravens forced a fumble deep in Pittsburgh territory and had the ball on the Steelers' 12-yard line. On two running plays and a pass to Rice, they gained only 8 yards and settled for a field goal.

The play of the game happened late in the first quarter. Jacoby Jones scorched the gridiron earth again. He fielded a punt on his own 37 and started slowly to his left. He saw a fissure in the coverage and blasted through it, taking a diagonal route 63 yards across the field. It would be the only touchdown the Ravens would score in the game. Jones now had scored touchdowns on returns three times—one from a punt and two from kickoffs.

The secondary played forcefully again. Corey Graham, signed from the Bears in the off-season, had an interception in Ravens territory and a key deflection of a potential touchdown pass intended for Steelers receiver Jericho Cotchery. The Ravens won a typical "grind-it-out" game against the Steelers 13–10 to move to 8–2 in the season.

The offense had struggled at Heinz Field. Flacco had been sacked three times. In his postgame comments, John Harbaugh took a page out of the great motivator and former Ravens coach Brian Billick's playbook. NFL Films captured the moment, and by Monday morning it had gone viral. "The toughest team won that football game," said Harbaugh. "The mentally tough team won that football game. The team that knows how to win won that football game."

The statement enraged Steelers coach Mike Tomlin, and he used it to incite his troops for the upcoming rematch two weeks later in Baltimore. The Steelers coach had led two teams to the Super Bowl, and both times they'd beaten the Ravens along the way. The fingers of the Ravens players, with the exception of Ray Lewis, lacked rings; they hadn't been to a Super Bowl since 2000 and hadn't won anything since Harbaugh had taken over. The Steelers used Harbaugh's postgame comments as their rallying cry for their next game in Baltimore.

The Ravens traveled to San Diego to face the Chargers on November 25. In 2011, San Diego had beaten the Ravens 34–14 in a dismal game. I hosted a dinner party for my neighbors and family that would have made my Italian grandmother proud. We had meatballs and crab cakes in Carolyn Bartoli's honor. But the game was over early in the third quarter and the guests left early.

In Week 12 of the 2012 season the Ravens trailed at halftime, 10–0. They had failed to move the ball deeper than the Charger 43-yard line, but the Ravens defense had stiffened against Philip Rivers and had kept the game close.

At the beginning of the third quarter the Ravens kicked a field goal to get on the board. It was now 10–3. At the end of the quarter the Ravens faced a fourth and 1 from the Chargers' 14-yard line, but Corey Liuget dropped Bernard Pierce for a 2-yard loss. Starting from their own 16, the Chargers then drove to the Ravens' 10-yard line, where former University of Maryland kicker Nick Novak extended the lead to 13–3.

With 7:55 remaining, the Ravens mounted a drive. Flacco used the speed of Jacoby Jones to loosen up the defense, delivering two passes for 42 yards. Then Joe switched over to Torrey Smith for three passes and 40 more yards. Dennis Pitta caught a 4-yard touchdown pass, and the Ravens were down by three, 13–10.

The Ravens needed to stop quarterback Philip Rivers and the Chargers offense. On third and 7, Rivers hit Ronnie Brown over the middle. Brendan Ayanbadejo, the Ray Lewis understudy whose number was 51 to Lewis's 52, wrapped Brown up and pulled him down for a 3-yard gain.

It was a play the Lewis would have easily made in his prime, but had he been playing on this day, Brown might have gotten the first down. It was just the type of play teams were using to beat Lewis in the middle of the field, where he had become a liability in third-down passing situations.

In the past, teams had refused to run screens or short middle routes against him, knowing that Lewis would blow up plays like that, but those days were gone. You couldn't run away from him because of his speed side-to-side. Even at 37, the aging linebacker could play defense against the run better than the majority of his contemporaries. But not short passes.

Still, like the ace of a pitching staff well past his prime—a Tom Seaver or a Nolan Ryan using everything left in the arsenal—Ray Lewis had studied the game of football for every nuance. He was determined to understand every formation, every intonation in the quarterback's voice. Now when he was there to meet the ball carrier, his play was based on instinct formed from experience and study rather than athleticism.

Lewis was also passing on his knowledge to Ayanbadejo, Dannell Ellerbe, and Jameel McClain. Standing in street clothes on the sidelines in San Diego, he vigorously encouraged his teammates, clapping his hands with every hit and positive play and yelling, "That is football man! That is football!"

The Ravens took over with three minutes remaining in the game. Flacco connected with Dennis Pitta into San Diego territory. Marshal Yanda committed a holding penalty on the next play and backed the Ravens up to their own 46-yard line. Flacco was then sacked by Antwan Barnes, and the ball came loose.

Fortunately, Michael Oher secured it or the game would have been over.

Facing a fourth and 29 from his own 37, Joe Flacco dropped back and lobbed what is called a checkdown pass—the last option for any quarterback under pressure and not the kind of play designed to net 30 yards—to Ray Rice, who had stayed in the backfield long enough to block and then had jumped out into the right flat.

Flacco saw the open area to the right, and seeing that it was his only option, put the ball into the hands of one of his playmakers. Rice caught the ball with 25 yards of space in front of him and a wall of Charger defenders across the field. They were in textbook formation, spread out, keeping the play in front of them. It was one against six, and all any one of those players had to do was tackle Ray Rice and the Chargers would have gotten the ball back. This was the kind of play that Rice saw himself making from the window of the New Rochelle projects he grew up in as he dreamed of playing in the NFL.

When the Ravens' sideline saw the pass, they groaned at first and then the play started to take shape. "I was thinking we needed a miracle," Terrell Suggs told the *Baltimore Sun*. "I was thinking we have Jacoby Jones and he can jump and catch it or we have Anquan Boldin with the best hands in the world. But then I saw [the] checkdown to Ray Rice and I thought he was going to pitch it."

Rice went 10 yards to the 50-yard line and turned, cutting sharply across the field where three Charger defenders lunged at him and missed. He noticed that the defenders "had started to flip their hips" and change direction. Rice picked up speed and from that point on kept his eyes on the first-down marker—barreling toward it.

With several Chargers in pursuit of Rice, at the end of his pass route Boldin raced back toward the play from the Chargers' 30-yard line. He managed to go a few yards past the first-down marker and deliver a crushing block that leveled Chargers safety Eric Weddle just as he was about to collide with Rice and prevent him from advancing any further. The block gave Rice just enough room to batter his way forward for an extra 6 yards and the critical first down. He landed on the ground between two tacklers with his helmet turned to the side, eyes on the first-down marker.

Rice had gained 2 yards more than what was needed, but it took an eternity for the referees to sort things out. It looked like his knee might have been down just short of the marker, and the replay would determine where the ball should be placed. When the officials measured again, the Ravens were back in business. They had a first down inside Chargers territory at the 34-yard line with 1:37 left.

As I watched from my living room, I announced to an empty house: "This is what champions do." The Ravens kicked a field goal to tie the score and won the game 16–13 in overtime.

"Checkdown," Rice said with a smile at the postgame press conference. "Hey-diddle-diddle, Ray Rice up the middle. That's just my little saying. That play was total will." The play defined the 2012 Ravens. They had suddenly become a team capable of rising from the clutches of defeat through sheer force of will, changing a game with one play. It provided a glimpse into the depth of the Ravens' resilient nature and how far they had come since losing to the Patriots the year before.

A loss against the Chargers would have changed the Ravens postseason course down the stretch. "It might be one of the greatest plays I've ever seen," said wide receiver Torrey Smith.

"I could have looked like a big-time idiot if we don't get that play," said Joe Flacco at the postgame press conference. "What the hell is he doing running a checkdown play? I don't think that will ever happen again." There had not been a play of that magnitude in Ravens franchise history up to that point—one that had so dramatically transformed a regular-season game from what looked like sure defeat into victory. "When teams win games like this, people start believing in the impossible," wrote Mike Preston in the *Baltimore Sun*.

There had been great postseason plays in Ravens history. The Trent Dilfer to Shannon Sharpe 96-yard "rip double slant" touchdown pass in the 2000 AFC Championship game against the Oakland Raiders was that kind of play—a knockdown punch in the early rounds of a prize fight that the Raiders never recovered from. Another big play was the 50-yard interception and touchdown against the Tennessee Titans the week before that Oakland playoff game, when Ray Lewis intervened between the ball and Titan running back Eddie George and barreled untouched down the sideline into the end zone.

I remember one play that stood out in the 1958 Colts championship game against the New York Giants during one of two spectacular drives led by Johnny Unitas, first in the waning moments of regulation to tie the score and then in overtime to win the game in sudden death.

On the first drive, the Colts needed 86 yards to win, not much less to kick a game-tying field goal. A John Unitas to Raymond Berry pass on second and 10 from their own 25 with 40 seconds left was more brilliant than even the Rice first down.

Giant linebacker Harland Svare had come up on Berry. Johnny had called a 10-yard square in, but that wasn't going to work with Svare in Berry's face. Unitas and Berry had discussed this situation years before, and now Berry looked down the line to Unitas and number 19 looked back. Berry faked left and Svare bit, and then Raymond ran an inside slant, just as they had discussed. The play didn't exist in coach Weeb Ewbank's playbook—and it gained 25 yards.

The impact of Rice's game-saving exploits in San Diego weren't truly felt until after the regular season had ended. As playoff scenarios began to unfold, the game at the very least helped keep the Ravens from missing the postseason altogether or from having to travel on the road throughout the playoffs.

Ray Rice was a fourth-and-29 type of competitor—someone whose heart and intensity made up for his size limitations. At 5 feet 9 inches and 195 pounds, the odds against his making it to the NFL had been high. He had grown up in a project known as "The Hollow" in New Rochelle, New York, the TV hometown of Rob and Laura Petrie on the old *Dick Van Dyke Show*. But Rice's life was no sitcom. Before Rice ever knew him, his father was shot and killed in a drive-by shooting that turned out to be a case of mistaken identity. All the running back possesses of his father is a snapshot that he carries with him.

Raised by his mother and a cousin nicknamed S.U.P.E. who was an aspiring rap singer and who served as a role model before moving to Los Angeles and being killed in a car accident, Rice escaped his situation by playing sports. He learned to play football on a narrow rectangle of concrete adjacent to a playground that had at its end an asphalt section that served as the end zone. By the age of 8, he was working odd jobs and bringing home money as "the man of the house."

This persistence was the trait that Ray Lewis latched onto in an effort to make Rice a leader of the team. Lewis sought out players whose work ethic approached his own and prized this trait above all else. There was also the bond they shared as two men who grew up without fathers. (Lewis's dad reappeared when the linebacker was 33 years old and an NFL superstar.) When Rice would ramble down the field headed for the end zone in front of the Ravens' sideline, Lewis would scream, "Go, Raymond, Go!" He yelled as though the young running back were his own son.

After starring at New Rochelle High in football and basketball, Rice attended Rutgers and left after his junior season to enter the NFL draft. The draft experts said he was too small and too slow to be an everyday back in the league. He was taken 55th overall in the 2008 draft and made it a point to prove everyone wrong. Since his first year he has had four 1,000-yard rushing seasons in a row. Writer Ryan Mink posted a story on the Ravens Web site about a young Ray Rice looking out the window of the projects one day after football practice in 11th grade. "Ma, I'm going to the league," Ray said. "I've got to make it to the league. I'll be glad when I can tell you, 'You don't have to work no more.'"

Rice remains devoted to his mother and has made sure she has everything she wants and doesn't have to work. But she still does work—using her skills to help special needs children.

Running on adrenaline, Ravens senior vice president of public relations Kevin Byrne got off the red-eye at BWI and headed home. He turned on 105.7, The Fan, in Baltimore to listen to *The Monday Morning Quarterback* with hosts Steve Davis and former police chief Ed Norris, ex–Baltimore Colt Bruce Laird, and Mike Preston, a columnist for the *Baltimore Sun*. The show provided objective in-depth coverage of Ravens games and could be brutal at times. "We're 9–2," said Davis, "and we could very easily be 1–10."

Byrne remembered the words of his former boss, Art Modell: "If the media isn't giving us a hard time then how will our fans know to believe them when things are going good." With that, Byrne turned the radio off. He was tired, and it had been a long flight. This was one of those times that Byrne wished he were still in Cleveland.

The Steelers returned to Baltimore on December 5, 2012, with revenge on their minds. Still seething from Harbaugh's postgame comments about which team was tougher, Mike Tomlin brought his Steelers into M&T Bank Stadium ready to play despite a 20–14 loss to the Browns the week before with Charlie Batch at quarterback.

I took my son Quinn (age 6) to the game, and we ended up in a sky box again, guests of a colleague from Johns Hopkins University Press. The box belonged to Crown Central Petroleum and its chairman of the board Henry Rosenberg. Mr. Rosenberg was a passionate Baltimore Colts fan before he became a Ravens fan and had tried to buy the Colts from Robert Irsay. "We had several conversations," he said. "He was either drunk or out of it. All I wanted to do was watch the Colts on Sundays."

Rosenberg had played a role in bringing football back to Baltimore, and he watched the Ravens with concern as they battled the Steelers. He noticed that Joe Flacco was keeping to himself on the sidelines after drives, sitting at the end of the bench rather than talking to his teammates.

Still, the Ravens led at halftime, 13–6. Just before the half, Flacco had tossed a perfect arching spiral to Anquan Boldin, who had gotten behind the defense for a touchdown. The roar inside M&T Bank Stadium was deafening, and my son held his ears. When the box door opened, it sounded like an avalanche outside. It looked like the Ravens would cruise to victory again over the Steelers.

Pittsburgh made some adjustments at halftime, and with Ed Reed playing a very deep safety, the middle of the field was wide open. Reed wasn't in the same zip code as the rest of the team. Charlie Batch fired to tight end Heath Miller over the middle and he ran untouched for 43 yards. It was as if a "gone fishing" sign had been planted where the linebackers should have been. Jonathan Dwyer bulldozed his way for 16 yards and the score was tied.

The middle remained open on the next Steelers drive, and Emmanuel Sanders caught a pass coming across the 50-yard line with only Ed Reed to beat. Reed's angle on the play was diminishing with each Sanders stride. The receiver was headed toward the end zone, but he somehow lost control of the ball and Reed recovered the fumble.

Ray Rice ran 34 yards for a touchdown, and late in the third quarter the Ravens took the lead again 20–13. At the end of the quarter, Batch overthrew a wide-open Sanders, alone in the end zone, for a score that would have tied the game. The Steelers had now blown two touchdowns that would have had them ahead by 7 instead of trailing by 7.

Despite his touchdown run, Rice would touch the ball only one more time in the game, in a 10-yard run for a first down. In the fourth quarter local news station WJZ caught footage of Rice on the sidelines, visibly annoyed with coach Cam Cameron and storming away from the interaction. Cameron was focused on his clipboard and didn't appear to engage the running back at all. Rice had been successful and he'd wanted the ball, but he received only five touches in the second half, none in the fourth quarter.

There had been times all season when Rice had disappeared from the offense. But this was the game after the fourth and 29 play when he'd stolen the lightning bolt off the Chargers helmet. He believed he deserved another chance to help win the game. The thought crossed my mind that the great play in San Diego happened because Rice never knew when he was going to get the ball and needed to maximize every chance he got.

With the Ravens ahead and the ball on their own 30, Flacco made another critical mistake against the Steelers. James Harrison sacked him and recovered the fumble. The old mistake-prone Joe had returned.

One player the Ravens have never been able to handle was the deceptively quick Steelers tight end Heath Miller. Now he tied the game with an acrobatic 7-yard catch-and-run touchdown. With his arm extended with the ball, Miller barely grazed the pylon with the pigskin before falling out of bounds.

This time Joe didn't bring them back. The Ravens offense died in the fourth quarter. Batch and the Steelers ran the clock out with a six-minute drive that ended with a field goal on the game's final play. The Steelers won the rematch 23–20.

After Shaun Suisham's game-winning field goal, John Harbaugh met Mike Tomlin for the postgame handshake. "Congratulations," Harbaugh said. Tomlin extended his arm without looking at the Ravens coach. He was staring straight ahead and moving fast. He didn't break stride as he moved toward the tunnel. "Hey, hey, hey," Harbaugh pulled Tomlin's hand back toward him and said something else. "Thank you," Tomlin finally responded, acknowledging the Ravens coach in a forceful and annoyed tone with bulging eyes.

In the postgame press conference, John Harbaugh was disappointed. "It was a very emotional game. It was a very disappointing loss. Lots of things could have been better."

As his players entered the visitors' locker room, Pittsburgh coach Mike Tomlin shook their hands, repeatedly saying "tough team" in response to Harbaugh's comments after the previous game in Pittsburgh.

The Steelers defense had shut down the Ravens offense during the fourth quarter. Charlie Batch had thrown for 276 yards, and the Ravens defense had failed to stop Pittsburgh late in the game.

Quinn and I walked out with the solemn crowd. We headed down Ravenswalk through Camden Yards to Conway Street, where my wife Christina and daughter Mary Julia were going to pick us up. I saw a father and son in a sea of purple wearing Steelers garb. The father had on a black jacket with gold sleeves and the white Super Bowl hat. The boy was my son Quinn's age, around 6 or 7, and he was holding his dad's hand. There were no other Steelers fans around. I tapped the dad on the shoulder. He had been walking with his head down and looked at me like I was the enemy and he was outnumbered. "Congratulations," I said to him. "The Steelers played a tough game tonight and deserved to win."

"Thank you, sir," he said. "You're the only person in the whole place that has said a word to us."

I remembered saying something once that enraged another team. My brother and I were serving as ball boys for the University of Maryland, Baltimore County Retrievers basketball team back in 1978. Our dad was the assistant coach. We were playing a game against hated crosstown rival Loyola College, now called Loyola University. As we headed to the locker room for my father's pregame talk we passed the Loyola team on the stairwell. My brother asked me who was going to win.

"We'll kick their ass tonight," I said. A few feet past the team, I heard one of their players ask, "What did that kid say?" Loyola scored 28 of the first 30 points in the game. I learned my lesson and never told my father about the incident.

In addition to Henry Rosenberg, *Sun* reporter Matt Vensel had also noticed a disturbing trend emerging with Joe Flacco:

> I haven't been overly critical of Flacco this season—maybe I should have tweaked him more—because I feel he has gotten to the point in his career where we don't need to scrutinize what he did every single game. . . . I'm more concerned with what he does in the playoffs, and I'm sure the Ravens, who have to give him a new contract at season's end, are in the same boat. But it's that maddening lack of consistency—not just from game to game, but sometimes from quarter to quarter, as we saw again Sunday—that leaves him open to his many critics, fair or not, locally and nationally.

Flacco seemed as puzzled as anyone else as to why the offense had stalled. Joe talked to Kevin Cowherd of the *Sun* about "putting ourselves in some situations that weren't good," and watching in frustration as "we hurt ourselves a little bit." Flacco was now not only shutting down in big games on the road but also doing it at home.

Offensive coordinator Cam Cameron talked about a lack of third-down conversions as the reason for the offensive outage. Whatever the reason, there were times during the 2012 season when the offense looked abysmal—mostly in the beginning of games—and others when they were unstoppable and capable of doing extraordinary things like gaining 31 yards on a fourth and 29.

Anquan Boldin snatches a touchdown pass—and the arm of the Colts defender.

Joe Flacco takes aim in the first half of Super Bowl XLVII.

MVP of Super Bowl XLVII Joe Flacco hoists the Lombardi Trophy.

Jacoby Jones eyes the pathway to the longest kickoff return, 108 yards, in Super Bowl history.

John Harbaugh and Steve Bisciotti look happy before the playoff game against the Indianapolis Colts.

Ray Lewis squirrel-dances one last time at M&T Bank Stadium before the Colts' wildcard game.

RAY LEWIS
RAVENS

ABOVE: *Ray Lewis and his bionic arm and Dannell Ellerbe stuff Frank Gore for no gain.*

LEFT: *Ray Rice avoids six tacklers and jukes his way toward a first down on fourth and 29.*

Ed Reed makes an acrobatic interception, falling back into the end zone with the ball in one hand, against the Texans in 2011.

Ray Rice eyes the first-down marker as he's finally brought down on fourth and 29.

Torrey Smith catches a touchdown pass against the Patriots on the day after his brother's death.

Terrell Suggs rallies the crowd in a 35–7 rout of the Steelers.

5. Under Fire

Every football player tells a story,
how he made the team, the wondrous desire,
the game first happening in the bones of his boyhood.

—SHIRLEY J. BREWER

THE BALTIMORE RAVENS beat the New York Giants 34–7 in Super Bowl XXXV on January 28, 2001. A few days before, *Washington Post* writer Tony Kornheiser published a column excoriating fans who had jumped on the Ravens bandwagon entitled, "D.C. Root for Baltimore? Only a Raven Lunatic." Kornheiser was incensed about Washingtonians rooting for a team that had "been playing in Baltimore for about eight minutes." He went on to say that the city needed to hate the Ravens.

I lived in the D.C. metropolitan area at the time and sent the *Post* a letter that was published in response to the column. I wrote that D.C. wasn't filled with Redskins fans either but "midwesterners on two-year assignments" who had told their parents they wanted to be president. I also threw in that Baltimoreans "wouldn't root for the Redskins if they were the last team on earth."

In retrospect, Kornheiser had been right. For example, the Callaghan family in College Park, Maryland, had been thrown into turmoil. Dennis Callaghan had been a Redskins fan since childhood, and he switched his allegiance to the Ravens when they, as he told me, "through sheer force won Super Bowl XXXV." His son Dan remained loyal to the Redskins. "My son wasn't happy with his father," said Michele Callaghan.

"I'd be lying if I said it didn't annoy me at least a little bit," said Dan Callaghan.

> I think with him I find it a little less reprehensible than with some other people I know. He is a huge Edgar Allan Poe fan, and Poe has obvious connections to the Ravens. I'm pretty annoyed with people our age (mid-twenties) who had to have grown up watching the Redskins but who switched to the Ravens when they came to town and won a Super Bowl relatively quickly. We feel that if you are our age and lived in [Prince George's] or Anne Arundel County, you should be a Skins fan.

Tony had also been right about me. I too was one of those fans who had jumped on the Ravens bandwagon. I hadn't watched an entire Ravens game in my life until the 2000 playoffs. There was no prolonged suffering that real fans of teams endure, the purgatorial fires of consecutive losing seasons that strengthen the bond. I had rallied behind the blue-collar quarterback Trent Dilfer. I cheered for Shannon Sharpe. I had leapt onto the purple bus because I was pleased for my hometown—a place I didn't know anymore. But I wasn't a Ravens fan.

I was convinced that authentic Redskins fans didn't exist in the transient metropolis of D.C. And then I met my first die-hard Redskins fan. Ashby Owen had worked as a letter carrier before he retired, and my wife and I lived two doors down from him on Walnut Street in Alexandria, where our daughter, Mary Julia, was born. Owen was a lifelong Washington Redskins fan. Every Sunday when there was a home game he put on his tan sports jacket, ironed white shirt, and burgundy tie and headed out to FedEx

Field. "I always dressed up. If it was hot, I'd wear a white sport coat. That's just me. I always wore a hat too," he said in a stately Virginia drawl. My favorite hat of his was a pigskin brown fedora with a red band.

"I had coffee with former President Richard Nixon," he once told me. "Nice man. We talked about the state of the world. I delivered his mail and he'd invite me in every once in a while." Mr. Owen started going to Redskins games in the 1960s. His last season on the 50-yard line at FedEx Field was 2012.

We talked football on his stoop once a week. "George Allen was the one who really brought the Redskins up," he said. "Mark Rypien was my favorite quarterback of all time. I liked him more than Joe Theismann. Sonny Jurgensen was good too."

Mr. Owen taught me about his passion for the Washington Redskins, which had nothing to do with how good or bad they were. Even during their worst seasons—and there had been many since Dan Snyder bought the team in 1999—there was little to no traffic on the roads during games; people stayed home to watch the game. The team's fan base had maintained their fervor for no good reason beyond the nostalgia for fullback John Riggins, an offensive line known as the "The Hogs," and the George Allen and Joe Gibbs Super Bowl years. I would watch the games because they were the only team being shown, and when Joe Gibbs came back in 2004, I took more of an interest. I'd never seen Mr. Owen happier than when Gibbs led them back into the playoffs.

I knew something about the Redskins from growing up as a Baltimore Colts fan. One Thanksgiving Day I had watched the Redskins in the back room of Fields Old Trail Tavern on York Road in Baltimore, where my father and grandfather would take my brother and me. It was a place where alcoholics with complexions like burned-out light bulbs would fish spare coins out of the urinals.

I liked Larry Brown and Charley Taylor, and every time somebody threw a wobbly "dying quail" pass in our neighborhood games of tackle football, it was a "Kilmer" for Billy Kilmer. In my great-aunt Carita's basement, my brother and I watched Dallas Cowboy Clint Longley bring the Cowboys back from the brink of defeat against the Redskins with four touchdown passes on a Thanksgiving Day in 1974. Everyone had left the game and was upstairs talking. We called them all back down when the game got close.

When the Colts left in 1984, Redskins games were shown every Sunday in Baltimore. "The station got flooded with irate callers," said former Colts color man Vince Bagli. Baltimore Colts fans weren't about to start following the Redskins. Older Colts fans remembered the efforts of Redskins owner George Preston Marshall in the early '50s to keep a team from coming to Baltimore. He had wanted to call his team the Baltimore-Washington Redskins to capture both markets.

Things had started looking up for Mr. Owen and the Redskins in 2010 when Dan Snyder hired Mike Shanahan to coach the team. "He's right out of the Gibbs mold," Ashby told me during the interview. "I think that Dan Snyder is going to turn out to be a good owner in the end, too."

In 2012 the Skins drafted a new breed of quarterback in Robert Griffin III, or RG III as he was called, out of Baylor University. One image from his highlight-filled college career that stuck with me was a midfield scramble that ended when he rifled a dart 60 yards into the hands of a receiver coming across the back of the end zone.

I had studied the Ravens' 2012 schedule and circled the game in Week 14, when they would play the Redskins in Washington. The game followed the Steelers contest in Pittsburgh and had the potential, based on what I had seen over the years after big games, for a letdown.

But with RG III having such a great year, the Redskins weren't going to sneak up on the Ravens. Defensive coordinator Dean Pees would have to develop a customized plan to stop the rookie quarterback.

Shanahan had constructed the 2012 Redskins around an RG III–led offense that included a running attack reminiscent of the coach's Denver teams. Shanahan's blocking schemes brought success for many backs he groomed to play in them. Burly halfback Alfred Morris, a rookie from Florida Atlantic, had already achieved success in the Shanahan system and would gain more than 1,600 yards in his rookie season. The head coach mixed his pro-style offense with the spread attack RG III used at Baylor.

In RG III he also had someone who could shift the field with the run option. The new offense was called the "run and shoot" or "the pistol." In the pistol, the quarterback lines up closer to the center—only 3 yards back rather than 7, as in the shotgun. The pistol also differs from the shotgun in lining up the running back behind the quarterback rather than next to him. The quarterback can read the defense but is far enough back to see the passing routes. It's a flexible approach enhanced by the "read option," where the quarterback reacts to the defense when the ball is snapped to determine whether to pass, hand the ball off, or run. It also gave RG III the flexibility to change the play at the line. A number of teams, including the San Francisco 49ers, were running variations of it. Its strains and derivatives would lead the Redskins into the playoffs and the 49ers into the Super Bowl.

With a record of 6–6, the Redskins needed a win against the Ravens to keep their playoff dreams alive. I had watched only one Redskins game all year but had been impressed when RG III took the snap in the pistol formation and ran 76 yards around the end for a touchdown. I had never seen a quarterback do that in the NFL.

His name sounded like a Gatorade drink. He was 6 feet 2 inches and weighed 217 pounds. At Baylor he ran track in addition to football—the 400-meter hurdles—and won the Big 12 championship and the NCAA Midwest Regional. From the moment he arrived in Washington, he took control of the team, the franchise, and the city. "Our quarterback is as hot as fire," Mr. Owen told me after the 2012 season. "All he needs is a couple more weapons on offense."

The battered Ravens defense was going to have their hands full with RG III. To prepare for him, practice squad quarterback and former Oregon University standout Dennis Dixon ran the read-option offense on the scout team during practice. "The difficulty in preparing for the Redskins is the fact that their offense is a little bit unconventional. It encompasses elements of the read option, the dive option, but it's also very conventional in the sense that they run all the things that [head coach] Mike Shanahan has been running for years," said John Harbaugh on the Friday before the game in his comments to the media.

On December 9 the Ravens met the Redskins in a beltway brawl at FedEx Field. The Redskins started fast and took a 14–7 lead, using a mix of Alfred Morris and passes to Pierre Garçon, Santana Moss, and Leonard Hankerson.

The Ravens defense eventually settled down in the second quarter and started getting stops. The Ravens offense also found a rhythm. Joe Flacco began to dissect the Redskins secondary. Joe threw for three first-half touchdowns. Anquan Boldin caught two of them and Dennis Pitta caught one to stake the Ravens to a 21–14 halftime lead.

Slowly, the Redskins crept back into the game. Flacco turned the ball over twice to begin the second half, the first one on a first and 10 from the Ravens' 46 after being sacked by Rob Jackson, who knocked the ball loose and recovered the fumble. The Redskins closed the gap on a Kai Forbath field goal, 21–17.

The second turnover hurt the most because the Ravens were on the verge of expanding their 21–17 lead. On third and 6 from the Skins' 11, London Fletcher read Flacco's eyes and grabbed a short pass intended for Ray Rice. Fletcher was the Redskins version of Ray Lewis and he played like it against the Ravens.

Anquan Boldin delivered one of his more tactical performances of the season. He caught three passes for 78 yards. Two went for touchdowns. After he caught his second touchdown, guard Bobbie Williams stopped by him on the bench: "You finished?" "No," said Boldin. The third catch, a 28 yarder, set up what looked like the game-winning touchdown—a Ray Rice 7-yard run. The Ravens led 28–20 with 4:47 remaining in the game.

On the ensuing kickoff, rookie Courtney Upshaw ploughed into kick returner Niles Paul at full speed and jarred the ball loose. David Reed pounced on it near the sidelines. Ravens announcer Gerry Sandusky cued the microphone to say his signature line when the Ravens had the game locked up, "The hay is in the barn!"

But Reed was ruled out of bounds when he recovered the fumble and the Redskins maintained possession. Washington had life, but not much. The Ravens defense had grown more resilient as the game wore on, and they were wearing down the Skins offensive line.

Now the Skins took seven plays to move from their own 15 to the 27-yard line. Flushed from the pocket, RG III had run 3 yards past the line of scrimmage when Haloti Ngata fell on his right leg and knocked the future of the Redskins franchise out of the game. "Ngata's injuring of RG III made me hate the Ravens even more," said Dan Callaghan.

Rookie backup Kirk Cousins from Michigan State came in. This wasn't good. I'd watched him outperform Wisconsin's Russell Wilson—now tearing up the league with Seattle—when the Spartans defeated the Badgers on a Hail Mary pass in 2011. Cousins's first play from scrimmage, a pass to Pierre Garçon, led to an interference call on defensive back Chris Johnson. On the replay, it looked like Johnson had arrived at the same time as the ball.

The NFL referees in 2012, replacement or regular, had watched the Ravens defensive backs closely all season. The secondary had a reputation for helmet-to-helmet hits, personal fouls, and defenseless-receiver penalties. The Ravens' physical playing style didn't mesh with the agenda of the new NFL. In 2012 the league had become younger and faster, with rookies RG III, Russell Wilson, Andrew Luck, and Colin Kaepernick leading their teams into the playoffs. Teams with high-octane passing offenses like New England, New Orleans, and Green Bay were exciting to watch.

Defensive struggles and injured quarterbacks and receivers meant more concussions and fewer and fewer eyeballs on television screens. In 2011 Saints quarterback Drew Brees broke Johnny

Unitas's record of 47 consecutive games with a touchdown pass. These fast-breaking offenses that focused on passing—what the league believed every fan and fantasy football stats geek wanted to see—resembled arena football.

The football being played by teams like the Ravens, Giants, and Steelers came under close scrutiny. The league was doing everything in its power to curtail helmet-to-helmet hits against defenseless quarterbacks and receivers. The possible long-term effects of concussions were being played out in the news as former players Dave Duerson and Junior Seau committed suicide. Duerson had asked that his brain be donated to science. Fines increased and intensified.

Bernard Pollard and Ed Reed had racked up "hits on defenseless receiver" penalties all season, and officials were sensitive to ensuring that the Ravens secondary played a clean game. The hit designed to separate the receiver from the ball as soon as he caught it, a key defensive play, was consistently being called a penalty.

Still, my father had always told me to play better than the referees on the basketball court, and his maxim applied here as well. In fact, play so well that the officials will not have a say in the outcome.

Back came RG III, hobbling on one leg across the field with a sprained knee. For a moment, I was relieved to see that Cousins was gone, but then RG III moved the ball from the Redskins' 47 to the Ravens' 26. After that sequence of plays, he was too injured to continue.

Kirk Cousins returned, and on a third down and with no blitz pressure from the Ravens, found Pierre Garçon, the former Indianapolis Colt, in the corner of the end zone for 6 points. Defensive back Chris Johnson had played too shallow, and Ed Reed was late getting to Garçon. The Ravens would be defending a 2-point conversion with the game on the line for a second time this season.

Redskins offensive coordinator Kyle Shanahan made the call of the year against the Ravens—one that no one expected. Cousins took the snap and headed straight for the goal line. By the time Ed Reed got there with a shoulder tackle, Cousins had scored.

The Redskins kickoff resulted in a touchback. Joe Flacco promptly took a knee to run out the clock in regulation. The Ravens would take their chances in the overtime period.

Why not take a couple of shots downfield and then run out the clock? Or better yet, why not try another checkdown play to Rice to see what he could do? Rice had made something out of a throwaway pass in San Diego, and it became the fourth and 29 play that led to a victory.

"What's disturbing about this loss is that with 29 seconds left—a lifetime in the NFL—the Ravens decided to take a knee, showing their unwillingness to be bold—or great," wrote Stan Charles in *Press Box.*

The Ravens were playing not to lose against their crosstown rival. In the extra period, the breakdowns continued. The Ravens went three and out with one pass and two running plays. Mentally, they appeared burned out, and the normally reliable Ravens special teams faltered. The punt team gave up a 64-yard return to Richard Crawford. The Skins had the ball on the Ravens' 24. Alfred Morris ran the ball three times, and Kai Forbath kicked the game-winning field goal. The Ravens lost a game they should have won, 31–28.

Baltimore Sun columnist Mike Preston wrote a report card after every game. Joe Flacco received a grade of C. "He still struggles with pocket awareness, and doesn't know when to step up in the pocket. Flacco started the season off strong, but has returned to his old form of being inconsistent—not just from game to game, but half to half." Preston gave the linebackers a D. He would have failed them, but according to his grading system you are eligible for a D in gym class as long as you put the uniform on.

John Harbaugh began the press conference by congratulating the Redskins. "We're not going to be disheartened," said Harbaugh in a video captured by reporter Jerry Coleman. "We understand what we are fighting for. I think we understand where we gotta go to get better as a football team . . . some things we have to, uh . . ." Then he paused uncharacteristically for a second, distracted by something on his mind, and considered what he was going to say: ". . . to do to be the kind of football team we want to be in December here."

He was struggling to reveal something that was about to happen and his answers were clipped. One reporter then asked him about the offensive performance in the second half, and he answered the question by first talking about how the defense responded well after the first quarter and then added hastily that he needed to look at the tape to answer the question.

The Ravens had scored 28 points against the Redskins but had been inconsistent in the second half and lost the game. The offensive line had done a poor job of protecting their quarterback when the game was on the line. Their offense was ranked nineteenth in the NFL.

In the biggest move of his five-year head-coaching career, John Harbaugh walked into offensive coordinator Cam Cameron's office at 5 A.M. on Monday morning December 10, 2012, and fired his friend, former boss, and one-time mentor. He would say that the short walk from his office to Cameron's was a painful one. "There is a very human side to this," said John Harbaugh, who was quoted in *Press Box* magazine. "Cam is my friend, he taught me a lot about coaching, and he is an outstanding coach. Personally, this is the hardest thing I've ever had to do as a coach."

It was a gutsy and unprecedented move. The Ravens still held first place in the AFC North at 9–4 when Harbaugh handed offensive coordinator responsibilities over to Jim Caldwell, who had never called a game before. The Ravens saw something in Caldwell—he was a natural leader who valued his players' opinions and ideas. He possessed the gravitas of a head coach but not the ego, and he had been a winner in Indianapolis. Caldwell understood from his experience in Indianapolis that winning was the most important thing.

"We have a motto we follow on this team: W.I.N.—What's Important Now—and what's important now is to find ways to get better, win the AFC North, and advance to the playoffs," said John Harbaugh in *Press Box*. "We needed a change." Joe Flacco looked to be regressing. He'd played tentatively on the road all year and had passed for less than 200 yards against both Pittsburgh and Washington. The shelving of the no-huddle offense had frustrated him.

Despite long-standing rumors that they didn't get along, Joe was surprised by Cameron's firing. "I was definitely stunned. I think as an offense we have to look at ourselves and see what we can do to be better. Obviously, we weren't good enough," said Flacco in the *Baltimore Sun*.

Ray Rice understood why the decision was made. "The expectation is to win around here," said Rice in the *Sun*. "We want to win. There's a reason why you put the Lombardi Trophy [banner] in the indoor facility. It's the only thing you can see. It's the biggest sign in here." Both Flacco and Rice appreciated that Cameron had been there to bring them into the league and develop them both into NFL stars. He had built an offense around Rice and Flacco beginning in 2008. They were now on their own.

With Flacco in a contract year, the organization needed to determine whether he was the right long-term choice for the franchise and whether or not Cameron had been hindering his progress in any way. With three games and the playoffs to come, there was still enough time to do that. All the fans who had flocked to the call-in shows had gotten their wish. The shackles were coming off Jersey Joe.

"There was tension in the relationship [with Joe]," said Steve Davis, sports talk show host on 105.7, The Fan. "Cam has his own way. He brought a bunch of quarterbacks into the league: Drew Brees, Philip Rivers, and Trent Green. All of whom had better success after Cam. Cam once told me in relation to Flacco, 'You try and develop a quarterback and win at the same time.'"

The wake-up call had come at a critical moment. The team was reeling after losing two straight games to backup quarterbacks in

Charlie Batch and Kirk Cousins. The defense was racked with injuries. Five defensive starters would be out for the Denver game, including safety Bernard Pollard; linebackers Jameel McClain, Dannell Ellerbe, and Ray Lewis; and cornerback Lardarius Webb.

Writing in *Press Box*, Stan Charles presented a scenario in which Ravens owner Steve Bisciotti had wanted Cameron gone after the Chargers game but Rice's incomprehensible game-saving 30-yard jaunt had spared him the guillotine. The Pittsburgh game had been bad but not awful—more of a defensive meltdown in the second half that could have been far worse from the scoreboard perspective if the Steelers hadn't fumbled balls or overthrown wide-open receivers in the end zone.

Firing Cameron then would have unleashed the mob on a crippled defense at the wrong time, and 20 points against the Steelers, the league's leading defense, is not an abysmal offensive performance.

The Redskins game, especially when the offense packed it in during the second half, proved that all ideas had been exhausted. Flacco and Cameron had failed in building an "elite offense" over the last five years, and with Peyton Manning on his way to Baltimore with his new wrecking crew, it was time to try a different approach.

Riding an eight-game winning streak, the AFC-West-leading Denver Broncos and Peyton Manning were coming to Baltimore. The Broncos had a 10–3 record, and after taking a season to recover from a neck injury, Manning had replaced Tim Tebow, who was now a New York Jet. They'd made the playoffs in 2011, but Manning's performance over 13 games had elevated the Denver Broncos into viable Super Bowl contenders.

The Ravens and Broncos were heading in different directions. The Broncos were locking up a number-one seed for the playoffs, and the Ravens were struggling after two straight losses to secure the AFC North Division crown.

A national tragedy occurred on Friday, December 16, and rendered everything else on that weekend trivial—including Sunday's NFL games. On that Friday morning, a disturbed young man gunned down twenty first-grade students and six teachers at Sandy Hook Elementary in Newtown, Connecticut. The entire nation—including NFL players—mourned the victims.

Ravens fan and first-grader Josephine "Joey" Gay was killed in the shooting. Her mother and father were from Maryland. She rarely left the house without wearing something purple. "Joey will forever be a part of our Ravens family," a team representative said in a statement reported by Jacques Kelly in the *Baltimore Sun*. In the aftermath of Sandy Hook, Baltimore had more important things on its mind than the Ravens and Broncos that weekend. At my son's basketball game early Saturday morning, one of the fathers told me he had been crying all night thinking about the children who had been killed.

On that Saturday afternoon, I went to pick up my children, Mary Julia and Quinn, at my son's kindergarten, Brown Memorial. They were making gingerbread houses for the holidays with a dozen other children in a classroom. I stopped as I walked down the hallway and listened to their voices—talking and laughing as they decorated their miniature dwellings. They were having a lot of fun squeezing icing over the rooftops and laying down sour belt shingles. They used peppermints for tiles to line the walkways.

I went in and sat down next to my daughter in one of the small chairs. With a lump in my throat, I helped her make licorice windows. I looked across the table at my son and thought of Jack Pinto, the boy who had loved the New York Giants. My 6-year-old son had just finished his first season of tackle football. Those Sandy Hook children had been his age.

I didn't care about the Ravens game anymore. Several fans I talked to were staying at home and not going to the game on Sunday. They were doing something with their families and watching the game on television. I had a friend coming up from Richmond to see the game, so I went to the game to spend time with him.

When I looked out across the stadium from the back of the end zone, there were purple rows of empty seats everywhere. I wondered if the no-shows were related to Sandy Hook. For those at the game, the atmosphere in the stadium lacked its usual urgency.

Jim Caldwell, the new offensive coordinator, looked down from the Ravens sky booth as he called the plays. He and Dean Pees, the defensive coordinator, were both sending plays and formations down to the field. The sideline now belonged to head coach John Harbaugh, one week after things had gotten out of control at the end of the Redskins game.

"Harbaugh and Cameron, according to sources, were involved in a heated exchange on the sidelines that carried over into the locker room after the game. . . . Both Harbaugh and Bisciotti were not pleased with the play selection at the end of the half and end of the game. Harbaugh was also not happy with the pass protection in the second half and wanted Flacco to be protected more," wrote Mike Preston in the *Baltimore Sun*. A former Indiana University and Miami Dolphins head coach, Cameron had stayed on the sidelines with his play card in hand and his headset on, making him more accessible than was necessary. There was a feeling that his stubbornness emanated from a belief that he was still a head coach in his mind. "Cam didn't listen to anyone," said Steve Davis.

The Ravens stopped the Broncos on their first drive and had great field position at their own 45-yard line. On a third and 1 from the Denver 46, Flacco fumbled and safety Rahim Moore recovered. Any momentum the Ravens had to start the game was gone.

Peyton Manning piloted the Broncos offense downfield with a dexterity that only Tom Brady could rival. On their second drive, from the 47, Manning used 11 plays to seize small parcels of the field at a time and kick a field goal. He looked from side to side, kicked his right foot like he was starting a motorcycle, and switched plays at the line to run and pass away from the pressure of Paul Kruger and Haloti Ngata.

Just before the end of the first quarter, Broncos running back Knowshon Moreno took a handoff and ran 20 yards for a first down. Ed Reed came up to make a tackle and Moreno hurdled the safety. Reed flinched, expecting to make contact with Moreno, but it never happened. The back, filling in for an injured Willis McGahee, had hurdled over one of the league's most vicious tacklers. Reed would say after the game that he was playing with flu-like symptoms. Whatever the diagnosis, the Ravens looked bedridden.

The Broncos jumped out to a 10–0 first-half lead. The Ravens defense held Denver on two successive possessions, and the offense went to work with two minutes left in the half.

Flacco found Jacoby Jones for a 43-yard gain. A few plays later he completed a pass to Torrey Smith, who was tackled at the Denver 4. The crowd was on their feet for the first time in the half, screaming for a touchdown to get back in the game. The clock showed 30 seconds left. If they scored with 20 seconds left, that was hardly enough time even for Manning to march down the field. "Take a time out," I said. "What's the rush?"

It was a crucial moment in a season that was dangerously close to implosion. Caldwell finally had the offense rolling down the field. A 10–0 Bronco lead approaching halftime was about to be cut to 3. Why not talk about it?

I thought of Butch in the seat next to me and the conversations we'd had about clock management related to Billy Cundiff's missed kick in the AFC Championship against New England. We should have taken a time-out that time too. Butch wasn't there; he had stayed home to watch.

Joe Flacco dropped back to pass and threw into the left corner of the end zone toward Anquan Boldin. The throw was a fraction late and lacked the normal zip that we were accustomed to seeing. His short throws in the last three weeks had started to sail on him while his long throws had starting floating.

Denver safety Chris Harris stepped into the passing lane and intercepted the pass at the goal line. Harris raced down the sideline. Flacco took off in pursuit, avoiding a blocker and cutting off Harris's angle to the goal line. But Joe ran out of field and his headlong dive at Harris's ankles as the Denver cornerback fell into the end zone was futile.

Ravens photographer Phil Hoffmann tells the younger shutterbugs on the sidelines not to get discouraged when they miss a play. All too often they'll beat themselves up as the player runs into the end zone. He encourages them to stick with the play because he says you never know what is going to happen at the end of it. You might catch something that no one else gets because the others had already focused on the great play. At the end of the Harris interception, Flacco gave the photographers a little extra to shoot. He put his head down on the field and stayed there on the goal line for a few seconds.

It was a rare moment of emotion from the quarterback during a challenging stretch in his five-year career. He had fumbled in three straight games. He had thrown interceptions but not a "pick-six" since the Houston game. For a few fleeting seconds, "Joe Cool" had let his guard down. It instantly became a national social media phenomenon known as "Flaccoing." The game was over when he put his head down. It was another ugly and demoralizing loss. The Broncos extended the lead to 31–3 in the second half before the Ravens put up some meaningless touchdowns late and ended up losing 34–18.

"This game sucks," Ravens center Matt Birk had said to one of the coaches on the sidelines, and NFL Films had captured the comment. There was no better way to sum up the afternoon. "We're a 9–5 football team and it feels like we're 0–14 right now," Joe Flacco told the *Baltimore Sun*. "That's just the feeling that you have right after a game like this. It's going to test a lot of things in us guys."

Ray Rice was still focused on Sandy Hook and annoyed with the fantasy footballers who were sending him tweets. Rice tweeted back: "If you feel like tweeting me about a loss or how I let you down in fantasy just un-follow me. My prayers and thoughts are with Newtown, Conn."

In the press box former Baltimore Colts announcer Vince Bagli, an honorary guest, held court with the reporters. He had a seat in the press box for every Ravens home game. After the Denver game, they talked about the team and where they were headed in 2012. "The writers told me this is a mediocre team at best."

Walking to his car after the game, Baltimore writer and filmmaker Charles Cohen witnessed a fan holding a lighter to Joe Flacco's number 5 University of Delaware jersey.

John Harbaugh's postgame comments demonstrated his substantial resolve. He knew he had just put a short-handed defense on the field that couldn't beat most teams in the NFL. Linebacker Josh Bynes, signed off the practice squad a week before the game, made 14 tackles. Harbaugh also knew he had put Jim Caldwell in a difficult position after firing Cam Cameron and that it would take the coach a little more time to develop a cadence to the play calling. As bad as it looked on the field against the Broncos, Harbaugh took the entire discussion all the way back to the sultry August mornings of training camp. "Every goal that we have, starting with our first goal—which is to win the AFC North—is in front of us. It is still there. And every dream that we have—which is the ultimate dream—is still available to us. That's what you keep in mind."

All of it was true, even with Eli Manning and the New York Giants, the 2011 Super Bowl Champions, scheduled to play in M&T Bank Stadium on the following Sunday. The call-in shows were flooded with irate fans who wanted Flacco's and Harbaugh's heads.

There was even speculation that 49er Alex Smith could be the Ravens' quarterback in 2013. Smith had been replaced by Colin Kaepernick—another "pistol offense" outlaw who could gallop and pass and blister the scoreboard with points in a hurry. There were many fans on call-in shows who believed the Ravens were not going to win another game—that they would keep playing for the AFC North Division crown and Cincinnati would take it in the last game of the season.

Ravens season ticket holders started listing their personal seat licenses for sale on Craigslist with greater frequency. With ticket prices going up every year in a bad economy, a team that couldn't get to the next level was no longer worth the expense. How long would the city support a Ravens team that didn't fulfill expectations? The window was closing on Ray Lewis and Ed Reed to win a championship. If 2012 wasn't the year, and it sure didn't look that way, it might never happen at all. The franchise would have to rebuild the defense without Lewis and Reed. A return to prominence could take years, even with Terrell Suggs playing linebacker.

As the negativity swirled around the Ravens, Harbaugh focused on the interior. He stayed at home with his players and began the healing process. He had worked his entire coaching career for just such a situation. Coaches earn their living during times of adversity, and there was no better person to lead this team through a losing streak than John Harbaugh. Nothing could shake his resolve or positive nature. He didn't have the relentless competitive edge that his brother Jim possessed, but John could harness the sheer positive force of his will at any time.

A couple of weeks after the 2011 playoff loss to the Patriots, Steve Davis had spoken with John Harbaugh. "He couldn't wait to get going on the new season. He had moved on from New England. 'That's over with. We're done with that,' he told me." Davis said that coaches don't have the luxury that fans do to dwell on games. They are back at it at 5 A.M. the next day.

The tension that weighed on Harbaugh from having to defend a moribund offense week after week had been lifted. He no longer had to answer questions with words he didn't believe. It was liberating and frightening at the same time because a shot at the Super Bowl still existed. Cam Cameron was out and no longer the scapegoat for an underperforming team. Everyone in the organization, not just one embattled coordinator, now owned a piece of the outcome. The whole team was under fire.

6. A Giant Win

We're coming back now,
. . . no easy wins for us
just scrappy, sloppy
"don't quit till it's over" ball.

—Melody Compo

I **WALKED AROUND** the upper-deck terrace of M&T Bank Stadium with the sharp light of a December sun setting on Ravens fans mingling in the concession areas before the Giants game. Trains rumbled by and traffic had slowed on Russell Street to the west. It was two days before Christmas and my wife Christina's birthday.

I had taken her to Gertrude's restaurant at the Baltimore Museum of Art on the Friday before the Giants game and given her a new Mac computer as a surprise. "You hid your love of the Ravens pretty good while we were dating," she had told me a few years after we were married. She—not football—is the love of my life and supports my weekly excursions to Ravens games despite being a Patriots fan.

I had no expectations for the remainder of the Ravens' 2012 season. The Broncos, Patriots, and Texans had emerged as the teams to beat in the AFC. The Ravens had backdoored their way into the playoffs the week before, clinching a spot when the Steelers lost to the Cowboys, but the division title was still up for grabs. This season felt like another one where opportunities would be lost. Maybe the Ravens could win a playoff game or two but it didn't feel like a Super Bowl year.

I stopped and watched the last few minutes of the Bengals-Steelers game on a television near a souvenir stand. The score was tied 10–10, and the loser was likely out of the playoffs. I didn't want to play the Steelers again in the playoffs under any circumstances and prayed for their hibernation to begin. If the Ravens couldn't beat a Steelers team quarterbacked by Charlie Batch, how would they beat one quarterbacked by Ben Roethlisberger?

Then, miraculously, Big Ben threw an interception with 24 seconds left in regulation, and the Bengals drove far enough to kick a game-winning field goal, clinching at least a wildcard spot in the playoffs. So far, so good. Still, if the Ravens lost to the Giants this evening, they would be traveling to Cincinnati next week to play for the division title—another unpleasant scenario. The reigning Super Bowl champs stood between the Ravens and a 2012 AFC North Division crown.

Since the late 1950s, the Giants had played a role in all of Baltimore's NFL championships except one, the Colts' 1970 Super Bowl victory over the Dallas Cowboys. Even that game had a slight connection to the Giants—Cowboys Coach Tom Landry had been the Giants' defensive coordinator in the late '50s. Much more directly, the Colts had beaten the New York Giants in 1958 and 1959 to win their first two championships, and the Ravens had routed the Giants 34–7 to win their first Super Bowl.

The 1958 game was the infamous 23–17 "sudden death" victory that helped establish the NFL as a big-time league. The game was televised nationally to 40 million viewers. "Prior to that professional football wasn't even as popular as professional 'wrassling' in America," said former Colts-turned-Ravens Marching Band leader John Ziemann.

The 1958 game between the Colts and the Giants played a role in my childhood even though it occurred five years before I was born. I picked up details from my father and read about the game in books with titles like *Great Moments in the NFL*. I learned about Frank Gifford's controversial run that came within inches of a first down along with Johnny Unitas's two-minute drill and Alan Ameche's 1-yard run to win the game. I heard about a 60-yard pass to Lenny Moore. The mantra of "Unitas to Berry" was always being brought up around the beehive dryers in my grandmother's basement beauty salon or at the dinner table.

It was the famous photo of Ameche's game-ending run, however, that I studied and studied and studied. Then I would put on an old leather helmet with a single bar, pick up a football, and jump over my bed pretending to be "The Horse," holding the ball between both arms amid the cheers of the Yankee Stadium crowd that I imitated as I crash-landed on the floor.

The Colts also beat the Giants in 1959 in Baltimore 31–16 to win their second NFL Championship, but it wasn't a close game and it wasn't talked about much by my elders.

Five years after arriving in Baltimore, the Ravens beat the New York Giants in the 2000 Super Bowl, 34–7. Learning from Bill Belichick, who had coached with the Giants before becoming head coach in Cleveland, Ravens GM Ozzie Newsome had modeled that Ravens team after the great Giants teams of the late 1980s. He had created a defense around Ray Lewis in 2000 that gave up only 970 rushing yards and 165 points the entire season—both NFL records. The offense featured a power running game with rookie Jamal Lewis and an experienced quarterback in Trent Dilfer who could make the necessary throws when he had to and knew how to manage a game. The Ravens used the Giants' blueprint to beat a New York team that was very similar to them.

New York's influence on the Baltimore Ravens went beyond the wins and losses of championships. The Giants had defined for three decades the type of winning organization that Steve Bisciotti's team was striving to become—and they wanted the Lombardi Trophies to go with it. The Giants had won Super Bowls in 2007 and 2011 under head coach Tom Coughlin—both against the Patriots and Bill Belichick. Both coaches had worked together under

Giants head coach Bill Parcells in the late '80s, and it was the Parcells model that provided the foundation for all five Giants teams to appear in the Super Bowl, as well as the model that characterized both the 2000 and 2012 Ravens. In 2012 there were similarities between Ravens linebacker Ray Lewis and '80s Giants Hall of Fame linebacker Lawrence Taylor, between running backs Ray Rice and Joe Morris, and between quarterbacks Joe Flacco and Phil Simms—both big, tough, and sturdy drop-back passers whose throwing motions were almost identical. "There are similarities," said former Giants punter Sean Landeta, who played on the 1986 and 1990 Giants Super Bowl teams. "Maurice Carthon was our Vonta Leach."

Besides Parcells, the first and second Giants Super Bowl victories can be traced back to George Young, who served as Giants general manager from 1979 through 1998. Young perfected the method of "drafting the best player available," a philosophy Bill Belichick adopted in Cleveland and passed along to Ozzie Newsome and the eventually transplanted Ravens. Both organizations continue to employ this approach in making draft selections today.

Born and raised in Baltimore above a bakery in an Irish neighborhood, George Young attended Calvert Hall College High School and played football at Bucknell University. In 1958 he took over the football program at Baltimore City College High School, where he first showed his traits as an imposing personage and legendary disciplinarian. He joined Don Shula's staff in Baltimore in 1968 and in 1974 rejoined him in Miami.

NFL Commissioner Pete Rozelle facilitated Young's move to the Giants in 1979, trying to end the 15 awful years the Giants had suffered since losing the NFL championship game to Chicago in '63. Young's reputation was strong enough for Rozelle to recommend him as a compromise selection that the warring Mara family could agree on.

In New York, Young made Bill Parcells head coach of the Giants, and they shared both an affinity for discipline and a vision for building a football team that dominated its opponents physically. The Merriam-Webster definition of "smashmouth," a term that began appearing in 1984 just as the Giants started playing well, is "characterized by brute force without finesse." The word would be used incessantly over the next several years to describe the Giants' playing style.

As a City College student who wrote for the school paper when George Young coached and taught history there, former *Baltimore Sun* columnist Michael Olesker had witnessed Young's disciplinary nature. At a sports banquet in Baltimore after Young retired in the late '90s, Olesker asked him how he had dealt with the millionaire superstars of the NFL. "You have to identify their weaknesses," he said. Olesker asked, "What was Lawrence Taylor's weakness?" Taylor had been one of the most ferocious linebackers in the history of the game. "He's terrified of his wife," said Young.

I had followed Lawrence Taylor and the Giants closely after I moved to New York City in 1985 for graduate school, often reading about them over an egg cream at the Mill Luncheonette on the Upper West Side. I had no team to call my own—the Colts had left for Indy the year before—but I had a personal connection to the Giants. I had played basketball with Giants punter Sean Landeta on the Cockeysville-Springlake traveling team in 1973, when I was 10 years old. Landeta was our center and he was as tall then as he is now. He was also our best athlete and had always reminded me of a recreation council version of Jim Thorpe. That was as good a reason as any for a displaced Colts fan to follow a team.

In 1986 I took a leave of absence from the graduate program in poetry writing at Columbia University and instead did my best to replicate the exploits of Giants fan Frederick Exley, author of *A Fan's Notes* and legendary devotee of various saloons across the city. I carried the book with me to watch games and often reread his portrayal of an obsession with Giants running back Frank Gifford that led him to follow Gifford from Los Angeles and the University of Southern California to New York and the Giants.

During this time I stayed with my cousin Noelle, who starred on a daytime soap opera on ABC called *Loving*. She was dating actor Alec Baldwin, who asked me one night over dinner, "What do you want to write?" I answered, "Sports." "Then do it," he said. I never forgot those words of encouragement, and more than 20 years later, I published my first sports article about Johnny Unitas.

Giants fans reminded me of Baltimore Colts fans—the old-timers who drank Ballantine beer and shots of Jameson in Blarney Stones. I enjoyed watching the Giants win the 1986 Super Bowl 39–20, beating John Elway's Denver Broncos. I also relished the Giants' 1990 Super Bowl season and the team's improbable victories over San Francisco and Buffalo. My interest in the Giants waned during the Dan Reeves years. I moved back to the D.C. area in 1997 and was a displaced football fan again.

The 2012 Ravens wanted nothing more than to follow the footsteps of the 2011 Giants to the Super Bowl, and defeating them would bolster their postseason aspirations and give them a second straight division title. A loss would bring the Ravens one step closer to playing all their playoff games on the road, dramatically decreasing their Super Bowl chances.

The 2012 Giants were 8–6 and desperately trying to nail down a playoff spot. They had been shut out 34–0 in Atlanta the week before and had fallen out of first place in the NFC East. Giants quarterback Eli Manning had played poorly, throwing two interceptions.

Eli was that quiet, scruffy kid on the other team in a pick-up game who wasn't chosen first when sides were picked but was the one who beat you every time. His pass to David Tyree in the 2007 Super Bowl that Tyree trapped against the side of his helmet and his 2011 Super Bowl toss to Mario Manningham inches from the sideline were two plays that won world championships. He was a gamer and had played reasonably well in 2012.

If the Ravens could hold the Giants to field goals in the "red zone," they might have a shot. I was afraid of what might happen to the Ravens if the Giants were on their game. The Giants' physical defenders, including Jason Pierre-Paul, Osi Yumenyiora, and Mathias Kiwanuka, concerned me.

Ravens coach John Harbaugh kept focused on the AFC North Division title after the Denver loss. He talked about the week of preparation on the team's Web site and how the Ravens were approaching the Giants. "It was a positive attitude. 'Fierce' is a term that comes to mind immediately. That's how I'm feeling. This is the time of year where everything is on the line. . . . We are very excited. We know we are playing a great football team. We know we're playing a team that is just as determined as we are."

The Ravens came out of the tunnel looking like harbingers of doom in their black uniforms, the first time all season that they had worn them. Strange as it was to see after a three-game losing streak, they had a swagger about them as they took the field.

The Ravens won the toss and deferred to the second half. On the third play from scrimmage the Ravens attacked Eli Manning. Danelle Ellerbe blitzed up the middle, coming from the linebacker position and timing the snap of the ball. Ellerbe slammed Manning for a loss. Though an official flagged Terrell Suggs for jumping offside, it didn't matter. The play had ignited the crowd and signaled to the Giants that the Ravens were going to be the aggressor. Manning seemed uncomfortable in the pocket for the rest of the game. He looked rattled, unsure. The Giants punted the ball away and the Ravens scored on their first possession.

Baltimore marched down the field in 14 plays and scored a touchdown on their opening drive. The Ravens had adopted vintage New York Giants "run-first" football. They alternated Ray Rice and Bernard Pierce on six running plays that gained more than 40 yards. They churned five minutes of clock. On one play, Flacco pitched the ball to Ray Rice on an option for a 14-yard gain, a rarely used play. Both Rice and the rookie Pierce would gain more than 100 yards on the afternoon. It was smashmouth football, Meadowlands style, and no Ravens coach would be answering questions after the game about why the running game had been abandoned this week. Jim Caldwell's offense made a statement.

On the second Ravens drive, air traffic controller Caldwell opened the airport and Flacco chucked a perfect 43-yard bomb to Torrey Smith down the far sideline that Smith stole away from cornerback Corey Webster. Webster had been erratic all season for New York and the Ravens exploited him. Flacco went in from 1 yard out for a 14–0 lead.

Trailing 14–7 to start the second quarter, Eli Manning dropped back to pass from his own 29. Haloti Ngata chased him down and dumped Manning for a 15-yard loss. Ngata had been battling injuries all year, but today he charged through the Giants line like a bull running the streets of Pamplona. His most spectacular play of the year stopped the Giants' attempt to get back into the game in its tracks. Momentum stayed with the Ravens the rest of the game.

Ray Rice caught a pass coming out of the backfield and ran 27 yards for a score just before half to extend the lead to 24–7. He would finish with 158 total yards. The defense shut down Giants receivers Domenik Hixon and Victor Cruz. Cornerback Chykie Brown played the best game of his career, roaming the secondary like a predator and breaking up Manning's passes all afternoon. He looked like a second Ed Reed on the field.

The Ravens throttled the Giants 33–14. They gained 533 yards and controlled the ball for 40 minutes. Joe Flacco threw for more than 300 yards. The offense converted 11 of 18 third downs, while the defense knocked Eli Manning down nine times and sacked him three times. They had demolished the 2011 World Champions, victors over both Green Bay and San Francisco earlier in the year and a team that had scored more than 50 points against the Saints just two weeks earlier.

The convincing win clinched the AFC North Division, ensuring a Ravens home game in the first round of the playoffs. It gave a jittery team confidence and showed that they could put three bad losses behind them. The game also provided a playoff atmosphere before the postseason tournament started. It was a very successful trial run and also tracked back to the aftermath of the 2011 season, when the Ravens spent the off-season believing they would have beaten the Giants in the 2011 Super Bowl. They won handily without safety Bernard Pollard and Ray Lewis, two players who would be back for the playoffs. Ray Rice told ESPN, "This was a championship game for us."

Joe Flacco had played a complete game against the Giants and had given one of the better clutch performances of his career. Flacco's passes were crisp and precise, and he had spread the ball around to seven receivers in the game. His recent string of fumbles and interceptions was over, and during the postgame press conference he talked about the significance of the victory as it related to the immediate future. "We believe we're this kind of team, and we're really going to see if we are. I think that we showed ourselves and we showed people today that we are that kind of team. We're here to stay."

It was a bold statement from the laconic quarterback, who won games with the same lack of emotion as he lost them. He had just played his best game of the season with an offensive coordinator who had been on the job for two weeks. When he spoke about "that kind of team," he was referring to one that could make it to the Super Bowl in New Orleans. The "kind of team" that wins championships like the one in blue they had just beaten.

"It was as if a cloud had been lifted over Joe's head after Cameron was gone," said Steve Davis of 105.7, The Fan, after the season. Flacco's performance against the Giants hinted at what was to come.

Former Giants quarterback Phil Simms, now an NFL commentator, has always been a Joe Flacco fan. Ever since Joe walked onto the Ravens practice field in 2008, Simms saw him as the franchise quarterback of the future who would lead the Ravens. "The thought has never crossed my mind that Flacco is not the guy," said Simms on SI.com in 2011. "He can throw it with anybody in the NFL. He is an imposing physical person out there."

The reason Simms liked Flacco as a player is that he saw himself in Joe. Simms was a tough drop-back passer from Kentucky who had played at Morehead State. Nobody had ever heard of him and he was booed when he was selected in the draft, but he had a strong arm and rarely strayed from the pocket—similar to Flacco.

The oldest of six athletic brothers of Italian and Irish descent, Joe Flacco played high school football, baseball, and basketball at little-known Audubon High in South Jersey, with an enrollment of about 500 kids. His high school football team never had a winning record.

On his senior trip to Disney World, he visited All-Star Sports and threw a football 70 yards through the uprights. He attended the University of Pittsburgh to play football and was redshirted. In his first year playing, he saw limited time behind starter Tyler Palko. He then transferred to Delaware. His best collegiate game came against Navy in 2007, when he threw for four touchdowns and more than 400 yards. His arm strength and accuracy were the attributes that impressed NFL scouts the most, but his low-key demeanor was also impressive. "I like to tell people, look, man, we raised him to be a CEO, not a carnival act," his father Steve Flacco told Kevin Kernan of the *New York Post.* "You're a quarterback, why would you want anybody to ever see you sweat? And when you throw a touchdown pass, act like you've done it before."

Simms had also battled criticism for most of his career until he won a Super Bowl, and he had endured the constant microscope of the New York media and the pressure from the fans to play better. He wasn't Dan Marino or John Elway or Joe Montana. He wasn't going to be selected for shampoo commercials. In head-to-head competitions, he outplayed them all. He was down-to-earth and never seemed to lose his cool—similar to Flacco. "He [Flacco] was a baseball player growing up," said John Eisenberg, who writes for the Ravens Web site. "It's one pitch after another. There are no real highs or lows."

I had become a Joe Flacco fan after his performance in the 2011 AFC Championship game. He had done his part to win that game and take his team to the Super Bowl. I had had issues with his sense of urgency in games in previous years, but there wasn't anybody in the NFL who threw a more picturesque and catchable ball than Flacco. "Joe Flacco's biggest strength is his ability to make any throw on the field," said Tony Pente of the Ravens Hangout message board. "He's a got a big-time arm but he's also pretty accurate. Cam Cameron's terrible rounded off generic routes cost him some completion percentages because receivers rarely got separation. When Joe gets time he's dangerous."

At Ravens headquarters, the much-needed win was huge. It rescued the season. "I believe they felt they could beat anybody after they manhandled the Giants," said Keith Mills, who covered the Ravens on radio and television for WBAL. "They actually beat up the Giants. And you didn't do that often to a team coached by Tom Coughlin."

Critically, the Ravens were now able to rest their starters in the last regular season game in Cincinnati. Their hard work had paid off, and the starters had time to heal their aches and pains. On defense alone, Bernard Pollard had five cracked ribs, Dannell Ellerbe nursed an ankle injury, and Terrell Suggs and Haloti Ngata were banged up. Ray Lewis was almost ready to come back. The injuries were beginning to heal.

Talented backup quarterback Tyrod Taylor played most of the Cincinnati game in a losing cause. A graduate of Virginia Tech, Taylor had a record of 34–4 as a starter. My Virginia Cavaliers never beat a Taylor-led team. During Taylor's rookie preseason in 2011, Ravens photographer Phil Hoffmann was talking to Kevin Byrne. "This guy has been compared to Troy Smith," said Hoffmann. "This is no Troy Smith," said Bryne. "He can do it all."

Taylor moved the ball and on one play rushed for 28 yards, making the Bengals miss tackles in the open field. It was exciting to watch him play, but he hadn't done much in his first two seasons and was a little rusty.

Cincinnati kept their first-string defense on the field, and Taylor threw a pick-six from inside his own 10-yard line to Carlos Dunlap with six minutes left in the fourth quarter, giving the Bengals a meaningless 23–17 win.

One incident stuck with me after the game. During the Ravens' first offensive possession on the third play of the game, Ray Rice got entangled with Bengals rookie linebacker Vontaze Burfict in the backfield. Rice's back was turned and he didn't see that the play had ended. He started and ended the minor entanglement by throwing Burfict to the ground in disgust and was hit with a personal foul. That was Rice's last play of the afternoon because Harbaugh most likely didn't want to take the chance that he'd get injured for the playoffs in fighting with another player. But the feisty running back's willingness to take on a trash-talking Bengals linebacker twice his size offered a glimpse into the Ravens' growing intensity. It was a meaningless game—but not to Ray Rice. He showed his team that he was going to fight for every inch of the field on every play.

The 2012 AFC playoffs were set. The Ravens were staying at home to play the Indianapolis Colts. Cincinnati would travel to Houston to play the Texans. Where losses to the Giants and the Bengals would have paired the Ravens with a Texans team that posed match-up problems for them in a hostile environment in Houston, the Giants win enabled them to enjoy the home crowd while facing rookie quarterback Andrew Luck. Still, it was a dangerous Colts team that had dedicated its season to a coach battling leukemia. Coach Chuck Pagano had been on the Ravens staff the year before and he had many friends in Baltimore.

The New York Giants continued their slide out of the 2012 playoffs, and at this point the Ravens appeared to me to have caught them at the right time. I wasn't convinced that the Ravens were poised for a deep playoff run.

As the season came to a close, I had neglected to recognize an emerging Ravens character trait. The Giants game had presented a must-win situation—if the Ravens were to avoid a very difficult road game, they'd have to win to secure the division. The Giants game also emphatically ended a losing streak. With their backs against the wall, the Ravens had forcefully responded.

7. Blue Horseshoes

. . . it isn't just Johnny she's mourning
but the slow stretch of Sundays lost, pouring
milk for us children, coffee for them,
and at game time, National Premium.

—Moira Egan

ON SUNDAY morning, January 6, in Baltimore, there was a light breeze and temperatures approached 50 degrees under a cloudless blue sky. I turned on my radio to listen to the pregame show on The Fan while getting dressed for the playoff game against the Indianapolis Colts. The somber keys of a piano played, interspersed with the voice of Ray Lewis. "I talked to my team today—about life. Everything that starts has an end. I told my team this would be my last ride," he said, fighting back tears. The news of his retirement was only five days old and the weight of it hit me. Tears welled in my eyes. This would be the last time I would see number 52 playing football in the Ravens' stadium.

The Ravens were about to face the Indianapolis Colts in a playoff game for the first time since 2006, when Peyton Manning and the Colts ruined one of the best seasons in Ravens franchise history. The Ravens had posted a 13–3 record that year, and the city believed victory against the team that left in the middle of the night was all but guaranteed. The Ravens defense frustrated Peyton Manning by intercepting two passes and keeping the Colts from the end zone, but the Colts defense returned the favor by picking off quarterback Steve McNair twice and preventing the Ravens from scoring a touchdown. The offense never recovered from a costly interception thrown from the Colts' 3-yard line. Indianapolis won 15–6, and Manning led them to their first Super Bowl victory.

The Colts had risen from the ashes of a disastrous 2–14 season in 2011 to finish 11–5 in 2012. Rookie quarterback Andrew Luck passed for 23 touchdowns and more than 4,300 yards. With veteran receiver Reggie Wayne and newcomer T. Y. Hilton running routes, Luck engineered a dangerous passing attack that could strike at any moment. He had an amazing knack for converting third and long situations by using his quick feet and overall athleticism. His performance began to dissolve Indy fans' memories of Peyton Manning, who had moved on to Denver and led the Broncos to the best record in the AFC. The pundits who picked the Colts over the Ravens in the wildcard game relished the thought of watching Manning duel against Luck in the following week's divisional round game in the Rocky Mountains.

"The thing about Luck is, that dude's not normal," Ravens strong safety Bernard Pollard told the *Baltimore Sun*. "I think just the type of player that he is, the guy stays calm all game long. Even if he throws interceptions or fumbles the ball, the guy steps into the pocket, he makes throws." Luck spent the first part of his childhood in London and Frankfurt and is an ardent follower of the Arsenal football club. He didn't start playing American football until the seventh grade in Texas.

The Colts also had selected a fiery new leader in head coach Chuck Pagano, the Ravens' defensive coordinator in 2011. Pagano had recruited Ed Reed to play at the University of Miami and maintained strong friendships with several Ravens players. Pagano had succeeded Jim Caldwell, the former head coach of Indy who was now a member of the Ravens' coaching staff and who had just been promoted to offensive coordinator after the late-season dismissal of Cam Cameron. Diagnosed in September 2012 with acute promyelocytic leukemia, Pagano had been forced to take an indefinite leave of absence from his coaching duties. Offensive coordinator Bruce Arians assumed head coaching responsibilities while Pagano received treatment.

The football media had billed 2012 as a rebuilding one for Indianapolis; the upstart Colts weren't picked to contend for a playoff spot. But with Pagano watching from a hospital bed, the Colts responded. Galvanized by their coach's illness, they began winning games. After starting the season 2–3, they won the next 9 of 11 to make the playoffs, beating quality teams such as Minnesota, Green Bay, and Houston—a team that had crushed the Ravens in the fifth game of the season.

After beating Miami 5–3, the Colts received a visit from Pagano, who had left the hospital to be with his team. He told the players they were already champions for defying the preseason predictions for a last-place finish. He went on to say, "My vision that I'm living, is to see two more daughters getting married, dancing at their weddings, and then hoisting that Lombardi several times and watching that confetti fall." Pagano rejoined the team on the sidelines for the regular season finale against Houston. The team's motto "Chuckstrong" served as a potent rallying cry.

On the Wednesday before the Colts game, Ray Lewis announced his retirement from the NFL at the end of the season. He said, choking up, "This is my last ride." Local radio stations in Baltimore celebrated one of the greatest football players of all time and the face of the Ravens franchise since its move to Baltimore in 1996. One caller shared that he had once asked Ray Lewis at a banquet why he wore number 52, and the linebacker told him that it was based on a deck of playing cards. As a young boy without a father, Lewis had explained, he would pull out a card and do that number of pushups. "It wasn't football that drove me to train," Lewis said in an NFL Films documentary about his life. "It was to stop my mother from coming home with bruises and black eyes."

In Baltimore, the Ray Lewis retirement eclipsed all other stories related to the game, including Pagano's recovery from leukemia. Focused on the legendary middle linebacker, I found it difficult to dredge up what felt like ancient Colts baggage. It was the first time I had personally seen the blue horseshoe against a pure white helmet in a playoff game since Christmas Eve in 1977 when the Raiders came to town. I went with my uncle that night and watched in agony as Oakland won a thrilling double-overtime game.

Now, in 2012, the Colts had become just another team on a glorious playoff afternoon. There were no middle fingers extended to the visiting team bus when it rolled into the lot, as had happened in 2006. I couldn't muster any of the old resentments against a team that had risen above the adversity of having a coach with a life-threatening illness. Still, former Baltimore Colts linebacker and Ravens announcer Stan White offered his own perspective on the game. "The revenge game was in 2006," he said, "and Chuck is a likable guy. Andrew Luck is likable. They had such a bad season the year before. I didn't hear too much talk about 1984, but I still can't get past the blue horseshoes."

Fans sporting vintage Johnny Unitas jerseys intermingled with Indianapolis Colts fans clad in the numbers of Luck and Manning. The immaculate sky over M&T Bank Stadium filled with boundless possibilities. I wondered what it would take from the Colts or any team to get Ray Lewis off the field for good. The retirement was certain to elevate the play of his teammates but what effect would it have on the Indy Colts? A new season began on the way to the stadium. A sense of gratitude hung in the air. We were gathering to say goodbye to the franchise's iconic player. There would be plenty of time to sift through the body of work after the season, including the complexities of a flawed superstar, but the final home game was about a football player trying to extend his season. The convincing Ravens victory over the New York Giants two weeks before had gone a long way to reinvigorate a skeptical fan base—but the game itself in some sense had taken a back seat to Lewis.

More than 71,000 made the pilgrimage from all around the Baltimore area and beyond to see Ray Lewis play one last time in person, including Sheila "Pickles" Miller from the Eastern Shore and her daughter Emily. Pickles didn't know where the stadium was and asked me for directions as we were leaving the parking lot. I pointed out Poe's grave and Babe Ruth's house along the way. She explained her attendance this way: "I had to see Ray's last game," she said. "We went online this morning and got tickets."

It was miraculous that Lewis was able to play after what had been billed as a season-ending torn right triceps in mid-October. Lewis recalled his phone call with Ozzie Newsome shortly after the injury on BaltimoreRavens.com. "Don't put me on injured reserve," he had asked Newsome. "[Ozzie] was like, 'What do you mean?'" Lewis had replied, "Trust me, I will be back." Today he wore a contraption that encased his right arm like a knee brace.

The star linebacker had lost a step in recent years and was considered a liability against the pass, especially on third down. But after 17 seasons, he was still better than most players at his position. He, along with defensive costars Suggs, Lewis, Ellerbe, Pollard, and Ngata, had missed games during the season. Healthy and rested for the first time, the starting defense now stood at the edge of the tunnel, ready to take the field.

The ominous pounding chords of Eminem's "Lose Yourself" launched the introductions, and the Ravens "red eyes" appeared on the Jumbotron. Announcer Bruce Cunningham belted out the names of the defensive unit. Ed Reed strolled onto the field before Lewis, shaking his head with a finger to his lips as the crowd thundered its customary "Reed!" for several seconds. Many in the capacity crowd pondered Reed's future with the team. Staying in the moment, he pointed back to the smoking tunnel in an attempt to quiet the crowd and keep the focus on his good friend. Lewis had fallen to his knees in prayer before his name was called. Then he appeared, his eyes blackened like Marlon Brando's Kurtz from *Apocalypse Now.* His famed "squirrel dance" had one more scheduled run for the hometown crowd. Dirt flew from a chunk of sod. He sashayed from side to side, thrust out his massive torso, and cawed like a Raven. The Blue Angels roared overhead at the end of the national anthem. He embraced NFL Commissioner Roger Goodell on the Ravens' sideline. We knew as Ravens fans that it would never be like this again. Then Lewis gathered his team around him for one last pregame war party, a ritual he popularized around the NFL. "What time is it? Game Time! What time is it? Game Time!"

The Colts went three and out on their first drive and punted. The Ravens drove to the Colts' 11-yard line before Ray Rice fumbled—his first of two on that day, and his first of the 2012 season. From the outset, offensive coordinator Jim Caldwell worked the Colts defense laterally. He moved them from side to side, progressing gradually down the field. Rice ran off tackle left for 3 yards. Flacco passed right to Ed Dickson for 24 yards. Rice ran left for 4 yards. But nothing was sustained, and the teams traded possessions in a scoreless first quarter.

Using an assortment of slants and quick outs, the Colts drove to the Ravens' 30-yard line early in the second quarter. Luck's quick release was faster than any I had ever seen. He barely took two steps before rifling the ball out, and the Colts receivers were difficult to defend on 5- and 7-yard patterns. Former Pittsburgh offensive coordinator Arians had developed a game plan that was the exact replica of past Steelers games, with quick outs to the wide receivers and pick plays right off the line of scrimmage. (In a strange twist, Arians himself had come down with an undisclosed illness and was watching from the hospital.) The drive came to an abrupt end when linebacker Paul Kruger sacked Luck, causing a fumble that was recovered by Raven Pernell McPhee. McPhee carried the ball off the field and presented it to Ray Lewis as if to say, "Take this ball, I just did this for you." The retirement announcement was paying off as a motivational tool for the younger players. "We made a commitment to each other," Lewis would say after the game.

Running back Bernard Pierce put the offense on his back to begin the second quarter and rumbled into field goal range with 31 yards on four carries. The rookie from Temple would finish with 103 yards on 13 carries. Justin Tucker's foot edged the Ravens into the lead 3–0.

Luck almost threw a pick-six to Ray Lewis on the Colts' next possession. With the field in a mix of sun and shadow, the ball landed in Lewis's hands, and he tipped it up into his helmet, then deflected it again before it fell harmlessly to the turf. The play would have resulted in a touchdown for the Ravens and was eerily reminiscent of two tipped Manning passes in the 2006 playoff game that should have been intercepted.

The Ravens scored their first touchdown following a 47-yard screen pass to Ray Rice that ended at the 2-yard line. He caught the ball in a crowd of defenders and darted through a seam down the right sideline. Flacco targeted two passes to seldom-used receiver Tandon Doss in the end zone, and they both fell incomplete. But Vonta Leach bulled his way in from the 2 and the Ravens led 10–3.

On third and 26 from the Colts' 41 with 29 seconds left in the half, Luck dropped back to pass. Under pressure, he raced up through the pocket to the line of scrimmage and uncorked a perfect strike to T. Y. Hilton for a first down in Ravens territory. He threw the ball from right to left across the field on a rope. It resembled a play that a seasoned Fran Tarkenton would have made for the Minnesota Vikings. Luck simply knew where his receivers were going to be on the field, and he created a few extra seconds to locate Hilton. Adam Vinatieri kicked a 52-yard field goal, and the Colts trailed 10–6 at half. It was scary to watch how quickly Luck could move his team into scoring position.

Jim Caldwell was calling his fourth game as the new Ravens offensive coordinator. After a 34–17 home loss to Denver, his efforts against the New York Giants had produced a 33–14 blowout. The season-ending loss to the Bengals was played more like a preseason affair and didn't really count, as many key players were allowed to rest. Now Caldwell's leadership skills were needed again, and he appeared to relax Joe Flacco and give him confidence. The ex–head coach had his own motivation, too. He had taken the Colts to the Super Bowl in 2009, but lost to the Saints. He still had something to prove against his former team.

The offense had begun to buy in over the last couple of weeks. Caldwell's protection schemes were more robust than Cameron's and didn't leave Flacco exposed as much. Cameron had liked to use an empty backfield formation that telegraphed to everyone in the stadium that the Ravens were going to pass.

The offensive line had also been retooled, with Bryant McKinnie being released from his season-long "doghouse" status to play left tackle. He had shown up to camp out of shape after promising that he would be ready. His slow gait getting to the line did not mesh well with the no-huddle offense Cameron had employed. He had played so well in practice that Ed Reed had been yelling, "Bring back B-Mac." But that was in the past now, and writers like Mike Preston of the *Baltimore Sun* who had been calling for this change to happen finally got their wish. Michael Oher moved to right tackle and rookie Kelechi Osemele went to left guard.

It worked. The Colts only sacked Flacco once, and the reengineered line neutralized Colts defensive stalwarts Robert Mathis and Dwight Freeney. This structural improvement helped change the complexion of the postseason, giving Joe Flacco the few extra seconds he needed to make plays.

In the locker room at halftime, one player voiced his frustration that the play calling had been too conservative. Receiver Anquan Boldin hadn't caught a pass the entire half and he was seething. The Ravens would later say that they had wanted to see what the Colts were going to do in the first half before opening up the offense. With Pagano on the far sideline, it was a fair point. He had intimate knowledge of the Ravens playbook, having served as defensive coordinator. The coaches understood his frustration. "They listened because he's not a complainer," said football commentator Syreeta Hubbard of TheNFLchick.com. "He is a leader and his words were taken seriously."

The veteran receiver who had joined the Ravens prior to the 2010 season to win a Super Bowl had been lost at times in Cameron's offensive schemes over the past three years. Cameron often treated Boldin as a last resort and didn't believe he could get separation from his defenders. "Boldin is never open," Cameron had told the coaching staff in response to why the receiver's number wasn't called more often, according to those close to the team. Anquan didn't fit with the flash and speed of the no-huddle offense and had trouble gaining separation. He performed the role of possession receiver on a team with speedy wideouts Jacoby Jones and Torrey Smith. For the past two seasons, the Ravens resorted to number 81 only when the game was on the line and they needed a score.

The Ravens received the second half kickoff and started play from their own 18-yard line. On the second play from scrimmage, Robert Mathis sacked Joe Flacco for a 13-yard loss. On the next play, Flacco dropped back to pass. He rolled right pursued by Colts defenders and stopped short of the Colts' sideline. It looked like he was going to throw the ball away and run out of bounds, but he launched a 50-yard bomb down the far sideline to Boldin, who beat Antoine Bethea and made the catch at the Colts' 41. It looked like a desperation Hail Mary but it was not. A similar "scramble play" had been called for Torrey Smith in the Ravens loss to the Patriots one year before, and the ball was underthrown or the play would have led to a touchdown. This year the play unveiled an aggressive, risk-taking approach that had been missing all year.

On their next drive, Flacco found Boldin again for a 46-yard strike down the sideline. It was a beautiful, big-armed Flacco pass—perfectly timed and placed into Boldin's hands. Then Flacco hit Dennis Pitta on a crossing pattern for a 20-yard touchdown pass to take a 17–6 lead with eight minutes remaining in the third. The Colts stormed back, attacking the middle of the Ravens defense with short passes. At 37, Lewis could still play the run but he struggled against the pass, and offenses around the league finally had a way to beat him. Luck drove the Colts 71 yards before the drive fizzled at the Ravens' 9. The Baltimore defense stood its ground, denying the Colts 6 points again, but Adam Vinatieri kicked a field goal to keep Indy within a touchdown and 2-point conversion at 17–9.

To start the fourth quarter, the Ravens sprung Ray Rice for an 18-yard run, but the ball was punched out from under his arm with a blindside hit, and the Colts recovered on the Colts' 29. Andrew Luck began a drive into Ravens territory by connecting with Reggie Wayne for 19 yards, and then running back Vick Ballard broke off a 24-yard run. Then the Ravens "red zone" defense stiffened again. The Rice fumble had no repercussions as Vinatieri missed a 40-yard field goal wide.

On the next series, Pierce broke free for a 43-yard gain. In a contrast of running styles, where Ray Rice slammed head-on into a hole whether it was there or not, Pierce on this play held back until his blocking fell into place and the big runner with deceptive and explosive speed blasted through the hole toward the end zone.

Then Flacco called Boldin's number again. Covered by Darius Butler, Boldin gained a half step in the right corner of the end zone. Flacco saw the one-on-one coverage and lofted a pass high and toward the back corner. Butler defended it perfectly, thrusting his right arm into Boldin's chest as the ball arrived. But blessed with vise grips for hands, Boldin locked onto the ball and Butler's arm as both players crashed to the end-zone turf. One photo angle showed Boldin's eyes fixed on the ball in his hands a full head and shoulders above Butler's hand.

The receiver with the mindset of a linebacker had elevated his game. Boldin caught the touchdown pass with a vengeance that suggested he would come down with the ball by any means necessary, even if he had to take the defender's arm with him. With his fifth and final reception of the game, Boldin had racked up 145 receiving yards, a new Ravens playoff record for a wide receiver.

This brilliant touchdown catch sent a message to his quarterback and to his team that he would catch any ball thrown near him. At the Ravens postgame press conference, it came out that Boldin had approached Joe Flacco before the game and told him he felt like he had 200 yards in him. "I just wanted to go out and give everything. I think everyone in the locker room wanted to make sure this wasn't our last game. I think we all have a goal in mind, and we're focused in on that goal."

With five minutes remaining Cary Williams sealed the victory by intercepting Luck. As the Ravens ran out the clock, Lewis came in for the final play, and Flacco was honored to have him in the backfield. Ray tossed in a bonus squirrel dance that miffed Colt Reggie Wayne. Then he took a victory lap around the stadium á la Orioles star Cal Ripken's tour after breaking Lou Gehrig's record for consecutive games played.

The Ravens had won a hard-fought game 24–9. It wasn't a work of art by any means. They battled and broke a few big plays downfield, and at other times they struggled. Nineteen games in and they still hadn't put together 60 minutes of football. They had beaten the Giants soundly two weeks prior by putting up 24 points in the first half but only 9 in the second half. Flacco had arguably played his best game of the year that day, but they could improve upon a few things like goal-line offense that would come in handy in the playoffs.

The Colts offense had run them ragged everywhere but the end zone, but the Ravens defense continued to uphold its stingy "bend don't break" mantra inside the red zone, and their veteran effort harkened back to the 2000 Super Bowl team and a record-breaking defense that only gave up 165 points all season. That team held opponents without touchdowns for long stretches. Lewis had played an integral role back then defending both the pass and run with an unbridled fury. He finished this game with 13 tackles—and a clear vulnerability to the pass.

The Colts amassed 419 yards but they didn't score a touchdown. They ran a mind-boggling 87 plays in the game, keeping the Ravens defense on the field for 37 minutes. With Peyton Manning waiting in the wings for the Ravens on the following Saturday in Denver, the prognosticators believed that the former Colt would carve up the Ravens defense and pass for several touchdowns. Lewis mentioned that he had already turned his iPad in to receive Denver game film because "it's on to the next one."

After the game, Ravens coach John Harbaugh addressed Ray Lewis, Chuck Pagano, and the city's relationship to its former team. "I think we're grateful for the opportunity to be here and to witness this historic moment in sports," said Harbaugh. "It seems like [Lewis] played really well. And, it wasn't just about one guy. Nobody understands it more than the one guy we're talking about. It was about a team. It was about a city."

This playoff game will be remembered as the moment the lingering Colts' abandonment issues went away for good. "That was thirty years ago," said Michael Olesker, the author of *The Colts' Baltimore,* referring to the loss of the team in 1984. The only Baltimore professional football player to come close to matching the impact that the great Johnny Unitas had on his team and his city had just played his last down at home. The sports talk shows had already chiseled Lewis's visage into a hypothetical "Mount Rushmore of Baltimore Sports" that included Unitas, Brooks Robinson, and Cal Ripken. Lewis had earned his place next to them. The Ravens will begin their 18th season of existence in 2013 and their first without Ray Lewis, a new era in which the Colts will be just another team to beat.

Harbaugh expressed his appreciation of this new age in his postgame comments. "I think we've gotten to the point here in Baltimore, maybe everybody hasn't," he said after the game. "Maybe there will be some people who will be mad at me for saying this, but we sure respect them [the Colts]. [Chuck] is a great football coach. He's a great man. They have a great football team. And that Andrew Luck—he's going to be around a long time."

Quietly and without a lot of fanfare, Joe Flacco had just become the first quarterback to win a playoff game in each of his first five years in the league. His biggest challenges lay ahead of him, but there was enough evidence to suggest that he, too, would be around for the long term.

Colts running back Lenny Moore had stayed in Baltimore after his playing days and still simmered over the team's move to Indianapolis. "I am a Baltimore Colt and my affiliation [with the Colts] stops there," he said. "I was working in the office when they moved everything out." Moore, like Johnny Unitas, had welcomed the new team to Baltimore in 1996. He is a Ravens fan and a member of the Ravens Ring of Honor. "I was happy for Ozzie Newsome and Ray Lewis after the game."

Ravens fan Betty Egan watched the game at her granddaughter's house. She used to work feverishly on Sunday mornings in her Catonsville home during the 1960s and '70s to have dinner ready before the Colts games so she could join her family in the living room. They would watch the first half over pretzels and beer, and the children had their own treats. Dinner was always served at halftime. She'd cook pork roast—her favorite—or chicken, turkey, or roast beef with all the trimmings. She had eight mouths to feed, including her husband, the children, and her in-laws, all of whom lived in her house. Her father-in-law, "Fast Eddie" Egan, had attended St. Mary's Industrial School for Boys a few years after Babe Ruth and had fashioned one of the slugger's old bats into an axe handle. Her husband, Michael, was a poet and a teacher.

After halftime, the family would take their meals into the living room and watch the rest of the game. If the game wasn't sold out, which almost never happened in the 1960s, they would listen to it on the radio. Back then her daughter Sionna, the Gaelic name for the Shannon River, went upstairs to play with her baby dolls. Now she's a diehard Ravens fan.

Betty vividly remembers a playoff game in 1964 when Jim Brown ran all over the heavily favored Colts, gaining over 100 yards as Cleveland beat Baltimore 27–0. "He had one of the best games of his career and I went into labor," she said.

She had dated a football star in high school and learned the rules of the game, and then the Colts came along. Before that she "didn't know football from the man on the moon." She went out to Western Maryland College to watch the Colts practice and flirted with Gino Marchetti. "Move over Blondie," said Artie Donovan, "I need to talk with Gino." Donovan lifted her up and moved her a few feet away. "That was the time I got picked up by Artie Donovan," she said with a grin.

Betty was there to meet the Colts at Friendship Airport (now BWI) when they returned from the 1958 championship game. She received a sticker there that she still has on her back door. It reads, "Baltimore Colts, 1958." (Her son Patrick has first dibs on the door.) She still watches the grainy videos of her favorite player, Johnny Unitas, on the computer. "He was magnificent. He always did the right thing. I loved to watch that man's style."

Betty's daughter Moira followed in her father's footsteps as a poet and now lives in Rome, Italy, with her husband, the poet and translator Damiano Albeni. They watch the Ravens via the Web, often into the wee hours in the morning. Albeni even favors the Ravens over his beloved Roma soccer club.

Moira has published three volumes of poetry, and her work has been selected for the *Best American Poetry* anthology. She wrote "An Elegy for Johnny Unitas" on the day he died to console her distraught mother. Those Sunday dinners were long gone and it was the end of an era in Baltimore, but Betty remembered.

And yet Betty enjoyed watching the Ravens beat the Colts in the playoffs 24–9. She no longer had to rush around in the morning making Sunday dinner for eight people, and she has moved past the heartbreak of the Colts' leaving for Indianapolis. She enjoyed the game, but the Colts had become just another team to beat. "The Colts don't bother me anymore because the Ravens are so damn good."

8. The Mile High Miracle

What if we do the impossible?

—Ray Lewis

RAY LEWIS played his last game in Baltimore on January 6, 2013, against the Indianapolis Colts, but his 17th season was not over. The Ravens were moving on in the playoffs. He took a postgame victory lap around the stadium and began preparing for the Denver Broncos.

Almost no one gave the Ravens a chance against quarterback Peyton Manning and the Broncos in the AFC divisional round playoff at Mile High in Denver. The Broncos had already won the game on sports talk shows and blogs; playing it was apparently just a formality. ESPN had published a photo of Ray Lewis on its NFL landing page with the message, "Thanks for the Memories . . . because Sunday was your final NFL win, Ray Lewis. Your career will end in Denver."

With a 13–3 record, Denver had one of the best teams in the NFL. The Broncos had a highly ranked defense and an even better quarterback in Peyton Manning, who was looking for his 10th straight win against Baltimore. The Ravens defense had stayed on the field for 87 plays against Andrew Luck and the Indianapolis Colts. If a rookie could accomplish that, what was Peyton Manning going to do to them?

The Broncos' stadium provided another advantage. Sports Authority Field at Mile High sits more than 5,000 feet above sea level, and adjusting to the altitude is a significant challenge for any team. It's one of the toughest places to play in the NFL. What's more, the Broncos had demoralized the Ravens in Baltimore less than one month earlier in a 34–17 thrashing. The betting line favored the Broncos by more than 9 points.

These factors seemingly spelled doom for Baltimore. The Ravens had managed only one victory in their last five regular-season games to finish 10–6. They had backed into a division title because the Steelers and Bengals were also losing games down the stretch. The merits of the Ravens' victory over the Colts were lost in the pyrotechnics of Ray's last squirrel dance.

"And that's why you play the game," my father told me as we discussed the Broncos over the phone early in the week. He was a former basketball coach who had a reputation for rebuilding programs, and he liked the Ravens' chances.

The "underdog" role fitted the Ravens' psyche perfectly and served to motivate them. They had lost four times in December and were far from being considered a Super Bowl contender. They had barricaded themselves in "The Castle," their practice facility in Owings Mills, and Lewis had challenged his teammates "not to listen to anything outside of our building" during a short week of preparation for a Saturday game. "Everything was stacked up against us," he would later say.

In response, the Ravens adopted a desperate "junkyard dog" mentality. Ray Lewis had removed the Ravens' 2000 Lombardi Trophy from the case, emphasizing to the players that they had an opportunity to make their own mark in history.

However bleak the prospect of beating the Denver Broncos looked, the Ravens were flush with "intangibles." The pending retirement of Ray Lewis had reinvigorated them. Their spiritual leader was taking players aside one by one and reinforcing their commitment to the game. He was quoting Scripture. Lewis paraphrased Isaiah 54:17, "No weapon formed against us shall prosper," sharing this mantra with the team. He challenged them not to listen to anything about the game outside the Castle.

John Harbaugh maximized the moment by allowing Ray to speak in the locker room before games and at halftime, something that wasn't the norm. Usually, players were permitted to talk only after the games.

The defense was healthy for the first time all year—Ray Lewis and Terrell Suggs were on the field together—and Bernard Pollard and Dannell Ellerbe had returned. In the playoffs Peyton Manning would be staring into the tinted facemask of Ray Lewis, not at practice squad linebacker Josh Bynes, who had played that position when Denver visited Baltimore during the season.

In the December meeting of the two teams, receiver Anquan Boldin had not caught a pass. It seemed unlikely that he would be shut out again. He told a *Sun* reporter that he was hoping to play the Broncos and that this time, "We'll make it different." Jim Caldwell, the new Ravens offensive coordinator, had been Peyton Manning's quarterback coach and also his head coach in Indianapolis. They had both been jettisoned by Indianapolis after a dismal 2011 season, and Caldwell, like his ex-player, had something to prove.

Denver linebackers Von Miller, Elvis Dumervil, and Wesley Woodyard and All-Pro cornerback Champ Bailey played major roles in the Broncos' having the second-ranked defense in the NFL. But their high ranking was suspect. They had played the Chiefs, the Raiders, and the Chargers twice each during the season—not necessarily the strongest offensive teams in the NFL—and had dominated them. Also, with Peyton Manning as quarterback, the Denver defense hadn't been on the field very much.

The Ravens arrived in Denver on Friday night to play the game within a 24-hour window to combat the effects of the altitude. The

Sun reported that this decision was based on the opinion of several physicians. Players such as Paul Kruger were concerned about being winded early in the game.

The temperatures were expected to be below freezing, and this became the one thing that gave me hope as the week progressed. Peyton Manning had never won a playoff game in temperatures below 30 degrees.

I also knew something else about the 2012 Ravens team. They had yet to put together four solid quarters of football. They had dominated the Bengals, Raiders, and Giants, but they still hadn't played their best game.

Two hours before game time, I went for a run with our yellow lab Sam to release the pregame tension. Sam is named after Sam Smith—the commander of the Maryland militia during the Battle of Baltimore in 1814, when citizen soldiers had defended the city against 3,600 rounds from a fleet of British ships. A stout defense has been an intrinsic component of Baltimore's personality for the past 200 years.

The temperature in Baltimore on Saturday afternoon approached 50 degrees and the sun was out. I jogged up the Stony Run trail in the shadow of the Cathedral of Mary Our Queen, where Colts quarterback Johnny Unitas and tight end John Mackey had been remembered in memorial services. I ran the football fields of the Gilman School, where former 1970s Colts defensive lineman Joe Ehrmann helped coach the high school team. I encountered several families who were on their way to watch the Ravens game at parties in their neighborhoods. A line from T. S. Eliot's *Four Quartets* came into my head: "Midwinter spring is its own season."

Whole families were wearing purple game jerseys—"Baltimore Tuxedos" as Under Armour CEO Kevin Plank called them—and carried trays of brownies and slow cookers full of chili. I ran past assistant state's attorney Doug Vey and his family and fiction writer Jessica Blau, author of *The Summer of Naked Swim Parties.* Ravens fans were gathering outside Alonso's restaurant and bar on Cold Spring.

For most of the run, I thought about the words of John Harbaugh after the Ravens' regular-season loss to Denver. He had said that everything the Ravens had set out to accomplish was still in front of them. Their dream of getting to a Super Bowl remained intact—and so it did, I thought, at least for a few more hours.

I also thought about two of the greatest football players of their generation facing off against each other one last time in a game that would end either Manning's season or Lewis's career. Manning's Colts had beaten the Ravens on their way to the Super Bowl in the 2006 playoffs. Now both players had overcome major injuries and were on a mission to get back to the championship. Manning sustained four neck surgeries in 2011 and missed the entire season. It was a serious condition that nearly ended his career. Some thought he was finished, and the Colts had released him before they had to pay him a $28 million bonus. Broncos general manager John Elway then signed him to a five-year deal for $96 million and traded Tim Tebow, who had led the Broncos into the 2011 playoffs.

Lewis had been injured against the Cowboys, but nothing would keep him from returning for "one last ride." He worked out in Florida while listening to reports saying he was done for the year. He became increasingly agitated watching his teammates on television, shouting instructions at the screen.

Both great players wanted to get to the same place—the Crescent City on the banks of the Mississippi on February 3—and for Manning that meant his hometown. It would have been a fitting end to the season after many had thought he was finished. Before the game ESPN analyst Chris Berman predicted a Ravens victory. Out of all the *Baltimore Sun* writers, the Ravens' harshest critic during the season had been Mike Preston in his weekly report card. But Preston also had the Ravens winning the game.

Peter Schrager of Fox Sports picked Baltimore to beat Denver. "I covered a Steelers team that rode a veteran's last ride into Indianapolis and beat Peyton Manning in the 2005 divisional round," said Schrager. "I was in that Ravens locker room on Sunday [against Indy]. There was a certain unity—a certain desperation—that reminded me of both of those teams." I dispensed with Schrager's prediction by telling myself he was just bucking the trend.

On the field in Denver it was 13 degrees, and it would drop to 6 degrees before the game was over. The photographers and videographers had stuffed their pockets with chemical packs to keep their fingers warm. They dressed as if they were climbing Mount Everest. There would be cases of frostbite, and the generators behind the Ravens team bench would run out of propane because the game took so long.

For the third straight year I had been invited back to the home of my neighbors Derya and Mary Yavalar to watch the playoffs. I packed up a tray of lasagna, dressed my kids Mary Julia and Quinn in Ravens jerseys, and headed down the street.

I had experienced bitter, season-ending defeats in Derya Yavalar's living room the previous two years but thought that three might be a charm, and the atmosphere inside his home was a football fan's paradise. A soccer fan from Turkey, Derya had adopted the Ravens and texted with family members around the world during the game. He resembled "the most interesting man in the world" from the Dos Equis commercials and offered cigars at halftime. When the Ravens scored, shots of tequila were passed around on a sterling silver tray, and Turkish cheers erupted.

Derya's wife, Mary, is also a huge Ravens fan, and the couple hosted 15 people, including kids, that afternoon. Too excited to sit down, I stood at the back of their living room drinking Diet Cokes for the whole game.

The game started badly for the Ravens. After getting one first down, they had to punt. Broncos return man Trindon Holliday caught the ball at the 10-yard line and ran to the right, away from the Ravens pursuit. The Broncos annihilated a phalanx of Ravens defenders, and Holliday turned upfield with only the kicker to beat. He sprinted 90 yards down the sideline for a touchdown. The Broncos had knocked the wind out of the Ravens.

Jacoby Jones fumbled the kickoff but recovered on the 6-yard line. The Ravens were backed up against their own goal line. On third and 8 from the 8-yard line, Denver was called for pass interference on Tandon Doss. An 8-yard pass to Boldin made it second and 2 from the Ravens' 41.

Flacco dropped back to pass and launched a high-arching bomb down the middle of the field, where Torrey Smith had streaked past All-Pro cornerback Champ Bailey on his way to a 59-yard touchdown catch. The Ravens had tied the game at 7 in less than two minutes. Flacco would say after the game that the team's mood on the sidelines after the Holliday punt return had simply been "It's our turn."

Manning went to work again from his own 20-yard line. His arsenal of wide receivers presented challenges for the Ravens. At 6 feet 3 inches and 200 pounds, Eric Decker was big and fast; Demaryius Thomas, also 6 feet 3 inches, was bigger and bulkier at 230 pounds; and Brandon Stokley, a veteran and former Raven, could find the nooks and crannies in the defense.

On third down and 6, Manning threw to Decker in the right flat. Chykie Brown came over his right shoulder as the ball arrived and tipped the pass into the air behind the receiver. Corey Graham caught it and ran 39 yards for a touchdown. The Ravens led, 14–7.

The living room became a Turkish soccer stadium, and we screamed, "Es, Es, Es . . . Ki, Ki, Ki . . . Eski, Eski . . . Gume, Gume, Gume!" The floor shook as we cheered the equivalent of "Here We Come! "Here We Come!"

The much-maligned Ravens defense had perhaps made their best play of the year, even though the replay showed that Brown had arrived a fraction of a second early. The momentum had briefly swung in the Ravens' favor after a disastrous beginning.

Manning now took over and engineered two long scoring drives to take a 21–14 lead in the second quarter. Each ended with a touchdown pass from Manning. Former Raven Brandon Stokley made a great play to keep both feet in bounds after beating Corey Graham on one of the catches, and Knowshon Moreno beat his college roommate, fellow Georgia Bulldog Dannell Ellerbe, on another. Peyton Manning had wrested the momentum back to the Broncos. They were driving into Ravens territory again late in the second quarter. Matt Prater tried a 52-yard field goal, but his kicking foot skidded across the ground, and the ball never had a chance to reach the goalposts.

The Ravens had the ball with 1:21 left in the half. Flacco connected with Boldin for 11 yards and Pitta for 15. With 43 seconds left in the half, he threw a deep pass to a leaping Torrey Smith, who caught it airborne with his arms extended at the goal line and came down in the end zone, tying the game, 21–21.

The Broncos ran out the clock with 35 seconds remaining in the half. There was a small psychological victory for the Ravens in that move. Though the Broncos were playing in front of their home crowd and were favored to win the game, Denver coach John Fox didn't see the need to make the old Ravens defense work in the freezing cold one more time.

The second half began as horribly for Baltimore as the first. Trindon Holliday fielded the kickoff in the right corner of the end zone and wormed through the coverage going from left to right and then burst into the open for 104 yards and another touchdown. Again, the Ravens' special teams had been burned. The Broncos took a 28–21 lead. Their special teams had scored 14 points. No team had ever recovered from two kick returns for touchdowns in the history of the NFL playoffs.

But again the Ravens absorbed a knockout punch and got up off the mat. With three minutes to go in the third, Peyton Manning fumbled as he was sacked by defensive lineman Pernell McPhee, and Paul Kruger recovered at the Denver 37.

Ray Rice took care of the rest of the yards between there and the goal line. He only gained a yard on first down but blasted up the middle for 32 yards on the very next play. He then ran for 3 yards and then 1 for the touchdown. The game was tied again at 28. He would rush for 130 yards on the day.

Peyton Manning put his team in front with seven minutes remaining on a 17-yard pass play to Demaryius Thomas. Dan Dierdorf, color commentator for CBS, talked about the Ravens defense running out of gas, about their valiant but failed effort, and about how Peyton had been too much for them. The Broncos led 35–28, and the game was slipping away from the Ravens. Denver general manager John Elway, the quarterback who had said "no" to Baltimore so many years ago, stood at the edge of the Broncos' luxury box in anticipation of a victory over that same city's team.

At the end of the 2011 season, Elway had pledged to develop quarterback Tim Tebow, who willed the Broncos into the playoffs with a limited set of skills. When Manning became available, Tebow was traded to the Jets. Now Elway could survey the field with the satisfaction of believing that his gamble had paid off. A Broncos victory was imminent.

As he had done so many times during the season, Joe Flacco called on Anquan Boldin twice for passes of 19 and 17 yards, and he carried the offense to the Denver 31. But the drive fizzled there after Dennis Pitta couldn't handle a low throw. The Broncos took over with just a little more than three minutes left and had a chance to retain possession for the rest of the game. Denver coach John Fox ran the ball five straight times, but with 1:15 remaining in the game, Denver was forced to punt.

At the Modell Lyric theater in Baltimore, comedian Jim Gaffigan was performing the early show. He could see people in the audience checking their smart phones every few minutes. He stopped during one of his routines to ask, "Okay, what's the score?"

Derya and Mary Yavalar had a dinner party to attend, and they were dressed and ready to go with everyone still in their house. During the next time-out, all the guests scattered from the Yavalars' home to watch the game elsewhere. I ran with the kids and my neighbor Rob Duckwall to Rob's place across the street from my house. We stood in his kitchen to watch the last few minutes of the game.

Flacco threw incomplete to Dennis Pitta. Then he ran for 7 yards, and the clock ticked down below 50 seconds. "I hate to say this, Rob, because I know you care a lot about the Ravens, but this isn't looking good," said Rob's wife, Caitlin, before she headed upstairs to get ready for an evening out. I was fixed on the television and not yet willing to concede.

With his breath visible in the air, Joe Flacco took the snap from the shotgun position and dropped back to pass from his own 30-yard line on a third and 3 with 44 seconds left. On the Ravens' sideline, Ray Lewis sat shrouded in a hood with his head down like a toll taker in a closed tollbooth. The end of his career was upon him.

Around Baltimore, people were on their way home from parties, unable to bear another brutal playoff defeat. Others stood in the doorways of bars waiting for a final confirmation that the game was over and the Ravens had failed for a third straight year.

Flacco saw a Broncos safety "just sitting there" and Jacoby Jones coming open down the far sideline. He slid through a gap in the collapsing pocket and sidestepped to his left before getting hit. Joe launched a rainbow pass down the far right sideline.

Jones had blown past Denver cornerback Tony Carter at the line of scrimmage and had slowed briefly between midfield and the Broncos' 40-yard line to see if his quarterback was getting ready to fire the ball toward him. Carter sprinted to try to catch up to the Ravens receiver but it was too late.

Broncos safety Rahim Moore had broken back at the start of the play, but he had been caught flat-footed for a split second, and he, too, had waited too long to make a move toward Jones. Flacco threw the pass beyond both Jones and the converging Moore on a hunch that Jones had the better angle to make the catch.

For a moment Rahim Moore resembled an outfielder trying to judge a deep fly ball about to carry beyond his glove. Instead of trying to get to Jones and hit him as the ball arrived, he tried to deflect a ball that was three or four feet beyond his hands. He flailed at the air, stumbled backward, and fell down. Jones had used another burst of speed, the one reserved for turning kickoffs into touchdowns, to reach the ball once it got beyond Moore's outstretched hands. He stopped and cradled it at the 20-yard line as if he were catching a punt, then ran untouched into the end zone, blowing a kiss to the sky on the way in.

Ravens photographer Phil Hoffmann was standing at the 20-yard line and watched the play unfold directly in front of him. "I could have reached over and touched that ball," said Hoffmann. He didn't get a picture of the catch, but the veteran photographer didn't give up on it either and captured an iconic shot of Jones in the end zone with his arms raised to the sky.

A volcano had erupted in the Duckwalls' kitchen. I let out several riotous yawps and rebel yells. This would be the first time I would lose my voice watching a televised game. The kids bounded upstairs from the basement, and Caitlin, dressed for a night out, came downstairs asking, "Rob, what happened?" After seventeen years of following the Ravens, her husband merely smiled at her and deadpanned, "They scored."

The Ravens had tied the game for the fifth time, 35–35. They kicked off to Denver, and the ball landed in the end zone as a touchback. Manning had 31 seconds to move his team into scoring position, but the Broncos had been stunned by the Jones touchdown and decided to play for overtime. Peyton Manning took a knee and Denver closed up shop. With the game and their storybook 13–3 season on the line, they chose to do nothing.

On the sidelines, NFL Films captured Terrell Suggs taunting the Denver crowd behind the bench, as he had been doing all afternoon. "Don't y'all wish at a time like this that you had Tim Tebow?" Tebow had spent the entire season warming the bench in New York, and the question, while vintage Suggs, was as preposterous as the Ravens' having tied the game.

The teams struggled through most of a scoreless overtime period. With five minutes left, on a third and 13 from their own 3, the Ravens faced the biggest play of their season. A Sam Koch punt from the end zone into the frigid air would have easily put Denver within 10 yards of field goal range.

Flacco dropped back and rifled a perfect strike to Dennis Pitta on a seam route down the right side of the field, and the tight end left his feet to make an acrobatic catch for a 25-yard gain and breathing room. Pitta's catch allowed the Ravens to shift the field, and when Sam Koch later had to punt, Denver ended up with the ball on their own 7 yard line, 93 yards away from a score. The Flacco-to-Pitta pass was mostly overlooked after the game, but it was a key factor in the outcome.

The Broncos moved the ball to their own 38. Then linebacker Paul Kruger came off the right end like a bear in pursuit of Manning, who was running toward the right sideline to avoid the pursuit. Peyton stopped and threw back across the field to Brandon Stokley, a pass he'd executed on more than one occasion during the season. It had even gone for a touchdown against the Panthers. But this time Ravens corner Corey Graham intercepted the pass, and the ball belonged to the Ravens on the Denver 45-yard line.

Ray Rice took a handoff and ran for 11 yards. At the end of the play, Marshal Yanda, the massive guard from Iowa, chased his ball carrier down and crashed into the pile, moving Rice and the ball a couple of extra yards, to the Denver 34. Time expired in the first overtime.

Kicker Justin Tucker was limbering up on the sidelines. In between overtime periods, Tucker ran out onto the field and practiced a field goal. It was not supposed to happen, and according to the rule book the officials should have prevented it, but it was not a penalty. When play resumed, Ray Rice gained 5 more yards to the Denver 29, and Tucker came out again, this time for real.

John Harbaugh was kneeling on the sidelines with his arm around Ray Rice as the ball went through the uprights. He then hugged the running back and kissed the side of his head. The Ravens had won one of the most exciting games in NFL history, 38–35, in double overtime.

After the game, his voice low and trembling and laced with humility, Ray Lewis spoke to the media for 30 minutes on a range of topics. He reiterated his biblical mantra, "No weapon formed against us shall prosper," and he said that no matter what happened, "We claimed victory on the sidelines." He applauded the loyalty of the Denver fans and talked about how he was in awe of Peyton Manning even while he was preparing for him. He was enjoying every last moment of his final ride: "to look at men's eyes and get everybody to buy in, and when you get everybody to buy in it's just so special when you see it, when it comes to fruition because then it changes perspective on what we should pay attention to, you know?"

Lewis had made 17 tackles, but he talked very little about the victory itself—only what it meant within the larger context of his life. "What if we do the impossible? Man says . . . it's not possible. God says, 'I do the impossible,' and for us to come in here and win, being 9-, 10-point underdogs, that's the beautiful part about sports. That's the thing . . . I will probably miss about my career . . . to listen to what people say you can't do. I've never been a part of a game so crazy in my life."

Lewis talked about how he was using his life as a football player to help others. He talked about the kids he'd visited at Johns Hopkins Hospital on the Thursday before the game. "A friend of mine called me, asked me to come see some kids, and when I walked in there and I'm looking at these babies who are unfortunate because they have to be there, and it just took everything away." He then told a story about the AFC Championship game the year before. "I made a mistake before, you know, before the AFC Championship, a very ill child I was supposed to go see before that game, I never got a chance to see him off, I never got a chance to say my last goodbyes to him, and this time when the call came I had to go do it." He'd put down the iPad and let the studying take care of itself for an evening. He talked about the city of Baltimore and his hope that what the Ravens had accomplished had changed someone's life for the better.

When he said that he had "made a mistake before," it was hard not to think about the events in January 2000 that had landed him in jail on a double murder charge. He was as complex a figure as exists in professional sports, and he was using another example to tell on himself and reiterate that his character was flawed. His legacy would forever be tarnished, but he understood the responsibility of the gift he had been given as a leader, and he was using football to have a positive impact on people's lives.

His "last ride" had not come to an end in Denver as the pundits said it would, but before the season was over he would again have to address his actions on the night in Atlanta when two men lost their lives and would have to face new allegations that he used a banned substance to aid in his rapid recovery from what many medical experts initially thought was a season-ending triceps injury.

As the press conference came to a close, Lewis passed the mantle of the team's leadership on to a quarterback who had just played the game of his career. Lewis talked about Joe Flacco. "He grew up today. In the tunnel I told him—you're the general now, lead us to a victory. You will lead us today. I'm just here to facilitate things. Lead us, man. And to look in his eyes, he had something different about him today. And I just wanted to encourage him."

In a season of incomprehensible twists and turns, debilitating injuries, the firing of an offensive coordinator, the planned retirement of the franchise's greatest player, and apparent wins that ended up as frustrating losses when time ran out, the Baltimore Ravens came to Denver and played their best football game of the year. "We're special because of what we've been through," said Lewis.

Peyton Manning had listened to Lewis and waited until after the press conference to embrace the one player who knew what he'd just been through. Manning had thrown the interception that had given Baltimore the game. There had been other games against the Ravens, including one in 2006 when Manning had been on the winning team and Lewis had experienced what Peyton was now feeling.

This was one of the great moments of the season—a rare glimpse at the authenticity of Peyton Manning not as a pitchman for Buick or Visa but as a champion who understood that this moment wasn't his. They spoke in muffled tones, smiling at each other while Peyton's two-year-old son Marshall played near them. Only one word from the conversation was within earshot of reporters like Peter King of *Sports Illustrated.* The two future Hall of Famers talked about their "respect" for each other.

Neighborhood streets in Federal Hill, Hampden, and Fell's Point were jammed with Ravens fans. At the University of Maryland Medical Center labor and delivery department, newborns were being named Raven. The next morning at the 9:15 A.M. Mass at the Cathedral of Mary Our Queen, Monsignor Bruce Jarboe told a story about the game. "I see a lot of purple out there this morning, and that was some game yesterday evening. I watched with two of my fellow priests, and as the game got exciting I asked if they knew CPR."

The local media were trying to name the Jacoby Jones touchdown catch. It had been called "The Charm City Chuck," the "F-Bomb," "The Rocky Mountain Rainbow," and "The Mile High Miracle."

Standing on the sidelines in Denver, former Colts linebacker and Ravens announcer Stan White had only been able to shake his head. He had tried to defend Oakland Raiders tight end Dave Casper, who had contorted his body to make the catch that helped beat the Colts in the 1977 playoffs. "All I could think of as I watched Jones run in for the touchdown was the 'Ghost to the Post,'" said White. "It reminded me so much of that game."

For many Baltimoreans, it brought back memories of the great comebacks led by Johnny Unitas. For a new generation of Ravens fans, it had been the greatest game they had ever seen. Now the Ravens were headed back to the place where their season had ended the year before—Foxborough—where they would face the New England Patriots for a chance to go to the Super Bowl.

9. Finish It

At any given moment, who is in possession of the down and who is pillion with the ball can be two different things. A nod of distraction, an intercept, a recovered fumble, a blatant steal. Write it down.

—Scott Hightower

On Saturday, January 19, 2013, one day before the AFC Championship game against the New England Patriots, Hall of Fame Baltimore Orioles manager Earl Weaver passed away at the age of 82 while traveling on an Orioles cruise. Earl's daughter Kim had once told me at an event honoring her father that he was sometimes resentful of the attention the Colts received in Baltimore and felt the Orioles had played "second fiddle" to the football team, even when the Orioles were a much better team. I had assured her that during the spring, summer, and fall months of the 1970s and early '80s we lived and died with the fiery manager's every move, whether he was smearing dirt over home plate to make a point to an umpire or installing Pat Kelly as a pinch hitter during a late-inning rally.

On that Saturday in January, with weather more suited to a baseball opening day, more than 18,000 Orioles fans had descended on the Inner Harbor for the annual Fan Fest. When they arrived at the Convention Center, Earl's number 4 jersey was displayed on the stage with flowers. "I started crying when I walked through the door," said Paula Ketter, an O's fan from Springfield, Virginia. Fans made pilgrimages to his statue at Camden Yards all afternoon, where the team had set up a large bouquet of orange roses.

The "Birds of Baltimore"—the Orioles and the Ravens—had both once been Browns. As a boy growing up in St. Louis, Earl had snuck into games to watch the Browns, and his Dad ran the cleaning business that laundered the Browns and Cardinals uniforms. As the Baltimore Ravens prepared to play the New England Patriots for the second straight year in a try for the Super Bowl, Earl's passing trumped the Ravens pregame coverage.

My in-laws were in town from New Hampshire, and we took them to the Walters Art Museum in Baltimore's Mount Vernon neighborhood in the heart of downtown, home to the first major monument to George Washington in the nation. The Curtins were Patriots fans who had made the same trip on the AFC Championship weekend in 2011, when my father-in-law had confidently predicted victory. He was quiet this time around.

Ravens purple surrounded the museum. Fans wore jerseys, and cars rolled by with purple flags. Storefronts carried Ravens banners. Peggy Hoffman, co-owner of the Minás Boutique in Hampden, had watched all her purple accessories disappear during the week before the Patriots game. Purple elbow-length opera gloves, cloche hats, beads, earrings, belts, and scarves had vanished from her store. "I was pretty much out of purple bling by then," said Hoffman.

As we stopped to cross Charles Street, I saw a Ravens bird logo emblazoned on the sidewalk. There were words around it, and I asked my daughter, Mary Julia, to read to me what it said. "Ravens, Team," she said loud enough for the in-laws to hear.

On Sunday, I stuck to my pregame ritual of a run with the dog, a shower, and a wardrobe that included my Torrey Smith jersey, which had brought good luck to the Denver game. I left the Patriots fans in my house and trekked down to the Yavalars' home, playoff central, with my two children and a tray of brownies. I was so preoccupied and nervous about the Ravens-Patriots game that I forgot to watch the NFC Championship game that preceded it. I learned that Jim Harbaugh's 49ers had won the game 28–24 when his brother John congratulated him from the field in Foxborough before the game.

I was concerned about two things as I headed into the AFC Championship game against the Patriots: the officials and Bill Belichick. I feared the referees would coddle the Patriots wide receivers as if they were part of a Fabergé egg collection—especially given the Ravens secondary's growing reputation for personal fouls. And I feared that Belichick's high-flying aerial circus and the team's hurry-up style would pose problems for a slow Ravens defense.

My fears centered on the game plans that "the Hoodie"—as Belichick was sometimes called in reference to the hooded sweatshirt with the sheared sleeves that he wore on the sidelines—might develop to exploit the Ravens' weaknesses. On defense, Belichick and New England could stop Ray Rice and Bernard Pierce by stacking the line and relying on massive lineman Vince Wilfork to plug the gaps. Linebackers Rob Ninkovich and Brandon Spikes could also cause problems. On offense, the Patriots played an up-tempo style based on precision and finesse, but there was always a chance that Belichick would resort to playing a more physical brand of football to drive home the point that he could run the ball successfully if he wanted to. He sometimes did things like that.

In their earlier meeting in September, the Patriots had moved the ball at will but couldn't score touchdowns when they had to. Belichick would certainly be making adjustments to his "red zone" strategy.

But the Hoodie also knew that good fortune had played a role in some of his biggest victories dating back to 1990, when he was the defensive coordinator for the Giants. His plan to stop the high-scoring Bills offense in the 1990 Super Bowl had worked brilliantly by goading them into running the ball when they wanted to pass it. But Buffalo kicker Scott Norwood's last-second 47-yard field goal attempt also had to miss its mark for the Giants to win.

In the 2001 AFC Championship, Tom Brady had fumbled the ball to the Raiders at a critical moment but was saved when the officials ruled it an incomplete pass, the famous "tuck rule" game. And just a year before, in a game against the Ravens, receiver Lee Evans had neglected to secure a touchdown pass and Billy Cundiff had missed a game-tying field goal. It pays to be both good—and lucky.

I went on the Marc Steiner Show, a radio talk show in Baltimore, and discussed the Ravens' chances. My intuition told me that the Ravens would win and the score would not be close. I had had a similar feeling when we faced Pittsburgh in the opening game of the 2011 season, and we had won, 35–7. If we got to Brady or made him uncomfortable, we could win the game and win it convincingly. My next door neighbor, Liz Trotter, sent me an e-mail after the show: "I bet Sizzle [Terrell Suggs] can't wait to get his hands on Pretty Boy."

On Wednesday night I hunkered down for my weekly ritual of watching the Showtime channel's *Inside the NFL* with James Brown, Phil Simms, and Cris Collinsworth. New York Jets linebacker and former Raven Bart Scott analyzed the AFC Championship Game. "The Patriot receivers know they are going to have to pay a toll coming across the middle. The Ravens have four 'goons' over there in Lewis, Ngata, Reed, and Pollard." I feared that the "toll collection" approach would lead to penalties, but there was an underlying message in Scott's remark. Baltimore's aggressive play wouldn't be limited to defending the Patriots receivers. The Ravens would be hitting everyone hard.

I felt encouraged that the 49ers had beaten the Patriots 41–34 in Foxborough in December. The 49ers and the Ravens, with the Harbaugh brothers as their coaches, played a similar style of physical football. New England had struggled all year with smashmouth teams like the Cardinals, Ravens, and 49ers—all except for the

Texans, whom they beat soundly during the regular season and the playoffs. The Pats would also be playing without Rob Gronkowski, their All-Pro tight end. It wasn't going to be a close game in my mind because one of the two playing styles would prevail.

As the Patriots were beating Houston 34–7 in the divisional round, Ravens linebacker Brendon Ayanbadejo tweeted incendiary comments about the Patriots and the gimmicks embedded in their offensive schemes. "New England does some suspect stuff on offense," he tweeted. "Can't really respect it. Comparable to a cheap shot b4 a fight." He also mentioned Belichick's alleged spying activities. The Patriots coach had been accused in recent years of taping other teams' walk-throughs. It was a dumb move for a veteran player to make; the Ravens had given the Patriots extra motivation to beat them. With the AFC East lacking any real competition in 2012, the Ravens had become New England's current hated rival. The Ayanbadejo tweets reflected a lack of maturity, and he apologized for them the next day.

The Ravens received their own motivational boost from Clear Channel Outdoor Boston. The company posted a countdown to Ray Lewis's retirement party on seven billboards in highly trafficked areas. "Ray's Retirement Party begins in 4 days, 2 hours, and 55 minutes" read the signs as they ticked toward game time.

The Ray Lewis Traveling Salvation Show didn't need any more wind in its sails. It had become its own alternative energy source. With tears in his eyes Lewis had delivered a searing postgame locker room speech in Denver that was captured by Ravens videographers. "David ran to fight Goliath. He didn't walk," he said, talking about how the team had never wavered on the Denver sidelines. Coach Harbaugh's head was lowered, and players repeated lines after Lewis as if it were a sermon. I was not much of a believer in the "team of destiny" story line because there was still football to be played—one loss and there was no more destiny. Still, Lewis had created a spiritual bond and a sense of urgency. The players and coaches were feeding off it. His message had worked in Baltimore against the Colts and again in Denver against the Broncos. Those same "intangibles" were in play as the Ravens prepared for New England. I believed in intangibles but not destiny. Not yet.

Lewis's prophecy in Foxborough the year before had come true. He had told his team after the loss, "The fact is, we gotta come back and go to work to make sure we finish it next time." The team now had the opportunity to "finish it" just as he had said it could if they all worked hard every day. Prophecy or not, the Patriots were as heavily favored against the Ravens as the Broncos had been.

Rarely in life did you get the chance to have a "replay" or a "do over," but after a year of sleepless nights thinking about what could have been, the Ravens had returned. "Take a look around. Take a look around. We been here before," Lewis barked to his teammates in the blustery New England air. They had gathered at the place where they'd left the Lamar Hunt trophy the year before. When Ed Reed came out of the tunnel during introductions, mic'd up for NFL Films, he was singing a Phil Collins song with a slight lyrical change. "I've been waiting for this moment for 365."

On New England's first series, Tom Brady went deep to Wes Welker. The pesky receiver broke into the open down the left sideline, but the ball sailed a bit. Welker went airborne, extending his body and getting both his hands on it, but he couldn't bring it in. Brady had thrown the ball with the wind at his back, but he was rushed just enough to make the throw slightly off target. It was still catchable, but his go-to receiver couldn't hold on.

Despite the drop, Brady dinked and dunked his way down the field to the Ravens' 12-yard line, using short passes to move the chains in a kind of Chinese water torture. New England's "no-huddle" and "quick snap" offense kept the Ravens off balance. The Pats had always excelled at taking what the defense gave them.

A key play occurred with five minutes remaining in the first quarter. Joe Flacco threw an incomplete pass to Anquan Boldin, and the rangy Patriots cornerback Aqib Talib was injured on the play and lost for the game. This loss significantly hampered Belichick's plan to use Talib specifically to stop Boldin.

The Ravens trailed 3–0 at the end of the first quarter. "They will not win kicking field goals," John Harbaugh said twice on the sidelines into an NFL Films microphone. The Ravens drove 87 yards down the field to take a 7–3 lead to open the second quarter. Throwing with the wind at his back, Flacco rifled the ball on a straight line 25 yards to Torrey Smith. Ray Rice scored the touchdown from the 2-yard line.

The Patriots responded with a touchdown drive of their own. They moved the ball to the Ravens' 1-yard line, where they executed a perfect pick play, and Wes Welker flashed open to catch the touchdown for a 10–7 Patriots advantage.

Defensive back Corey Graham was visibly upset, and he got into a heated discussion with cornerback Chykie Brown. Lewis brought the defense together on the sideline. "We in a heavyweight fight. No more arguing. Things are gonna happen. We need everybody's positive energy, man. We in a championship fight. Let's play championship ball."

The next Ravens drive fizzled, and the Patriots were on the move again. On fourth and 1 from the Ravens' 34, Brady barked out signals and tapped the side of his helmet, distracting the defense. The ball was direct-snapped to Danny Woodhead, who ran 7 yards to the Ravens' 27. Here was the trickery that Ayanbadejo had tweeted about.

The Ravens defense forced a third and 10, and Brady fired a pass to Aaron Hernandez in the right flat that went for 17 yards. They had the ball on the Ravens' 10-yard line with 26 seconds left, with a real chance to extend the lead to 10 points before halftime.

Brady dropped back to pass and drifted to his left, looking into the end zone. Nobody was open. As he started running toward the goal line, Ed Reed raced up to stop him. The one safety in the NFL that could read a quarterback's eyes better than anyone else, who had wanted nothing more than to go to New Orleans to play a Super Bowl close to where he had grown up, was bearing down on the Patriots' superstar. Seeing he wouldn't make it before receiving an open-field hit from Reed, Brady fell into a slide at the 7-yard line. As Reed leaped in the air to avoid trampling on him, Brady kicked his right leg up at Reed to block the safety's fall. Reed flew over Brady and was slow getting up. It was clearly a personal foul, but the officials looked the other way.

"He kicked him!" Harbaugh pleaded his case on the sidelines. Brady walked over to Reed after the play was over and apologized. The Ravens were enraged—and motivated.

In the confusion, Brady and Belichick had lost track of time and the clock ran down to four seconds. It was a rare lapse in time management by the Patriots, and they were forced to kick a field goal. The Ravens had again held them to only 3 points.

Down 13–7 at halftime, the Ravens players and coaches were frustrated and boisterous according to team photographer Phil Hoffmann. They were saying, "How can this team be beating us? We are better than these guys." The general sentiment in the locker room was, "We didn't come here to play not to lose." It had been a raucous exchange, with Harbaugh echoing their sentiments.

In the spirit of the "championship fight" analogy Ray Lewis had used when exhorting his teammates to perform, Bernard Pollard was about to deliver the equivalent of a technical knockout, two punishing blows that had an impact on the outcome of the game. The first occurred on the opening drive of the second half. From his own 25, Brady threw to Wes Welker downfield and to the right. Welker caught the ball and was leveled by Pollard with a helmet-to-helmet hit that was accurately called unnecessary roughness.

The play netted 39 yards with the penalty, and the Pats had the ball on the Ravens' 36. Two plays later, Brady went back to Welker on a third and 8. The ball hit his hands as he was falling back and he dropped the pass. It was a key play in a game that had been controlled by the Patriots offense to that point, and it would have given New England a first down at the Ravens' 25-yard line. As the ball came to Welker, he saw monstrous defensive end Paul Kruger on the verge of tackling him, and it looked like the smaller receiver was anticipating the hit as the ball caromed off his hands. Did Pollard's hit three plays earlier play a role? It certainly didn't make Welker any less concerned about getting hit.

In a debatable decision, Belichick now opted not to attempt a 52-yard field goal and chose to play instead for field position. If kicker Stephen Gostkowski had missed a field goal, the Ravens would have had great field position. Instead, punter Zoltan Mesko pinned the Ravens on their own 13-yard line.

Sooner or later Brady was going to catch fire, and his receivers would start making plays. The Patriots would eventually find the end zone. The Ravens had to start winning the game. John Harbaugh was walking down the sidelines with 10 minutes to go in the third quarter. "Open it up," he told his offensive coordinator Jim Caldwell "or we'll lose this game."

Flacco used 11 plays to drive down the field and score. He connected with Dennis Pitta three times on the drive—the last catch for a 5-yard touchdown. The big tight end from Brigham Young who played like a wide receiver was becoming a favorite target. On the next drive, the Ravens scored another touchdown. This time Anquan Boldin, Torrey Smith, and Bernard Pierce contributed big plays. Flacco lobbed a "jump ball" to Boldin from 3 yards out, and the Ravens led 21–13 at the start of the fourth quarter.

Then Bernard Pollard lowered the boom again. Patriots running back Stevan Ridley took a handoff, went through a big hole around right end, and had gained 7 yards before Pollard met him near the Patriots' 40-yard line. Seeing Pollard coming in from the right, Ridley lowered his helmet to hit him. Pollard launched himself into the running back with an uppercut using his shoulder and helmet.

The crushing hit spun Ridley around 360 degrees and knocked the running back into a sitting position. He crumpled to the ground with a concussion that took him out of the game. Just before Ridley's backside touched the ground, the ball tumbled off his shin and out of his grasp. Dannell Ellerbe pounced on it first. "You got it Ell," said Reed before trying to dive under the bodies.

"You got it. Just hold on." A massive scrum ensued. Ravens defensive end Arthur Jones eventually emerged from the pile with the ball in his hand.

It was a hit that dramatically altered the course of the game. "That was the turning point of the football game there on the 40-yard line," Ravens coach John Harbaugh told the *Baltimore Sun.* "It was a tremendous hit. It was football at its finest. It was Bernard Pollard making a great physical tackle, just as good a tackle as you're ever going to see in football right there. That probably turned the game around right there."

Flacco sniffed blood in the water and he moved in for the kill. He found Torrey Smith for 16 yards. Then Joe did something he has done only a few times in his career. He dropped back and trotted around left end for 14 yards, almost tiptoeing on his way to a first down.

Joe tossed another "jump ball," an inside seam route to Boldin, who leaped in the air and brought it down while falling backward in the end zone. It was an "alley-oop" basketball play that Flacco and Boldin had worked on in practice, and ball placement was the key. Flacco's pass to a spot where only Anquan could grab it was quickly becoming a signature play.

The former Arizona Cardinals receiver had caught three touchdown passes in three playoff games—nearly equaling his total of four in 16 regular-season games. After the season, Ravens senior vice president Kevin Byrne said the Ravens had discovered "the best rebounder on the team" in Anquan Boldin.

"Jersey Joe is going for the throat," said Ravens radio announcer Gerry Sandusky. Flacco had put up 21 points to give the Ravens a 28–13 lead. Since 2008, the unit had never been characterized as one that would "go for the throat." During the 2012 season it had lacked consistency, and finishing off opponents had been an issue in Washington and at home against Pittsburgh with Cam Cameron in control of the offense. The Ravens had come from behind five times against Denver, but in this game Jim Caldwell's offense had continued to put the pressure on.

New England was beginning to wilt but they were far from finished. Brady drove his team to the Ravens' 19 and, under pressure on fourth down, threw a wobbling duck that fell harmlessly into the end zone. The Patriots defense sacked Flacco on the next series and forced a punt. Brady found Welker for 36 yards down the left sideline, and they were on the verge of scoring again. On the next play, Brady was looking into the end zone when Ravens defensive lineman Pernell McPhee was blocked into his passing lane.

McPhee was having a disappointing, injury-plagued sophomore season, after a rookie year in 2011 when he finished second on the team with six sacks. During the past year he had also dealt with the murder of his sister, the loss of a cousin, and the death of his godfather.

As Brady released the ball, the 6-foot-3-inch 280-pound McPhee reached high over the line and batted the pass into the air. It sputtered up like a field-goal kick 10 yards beyond the line of scrimmage, and linebacker Dannell Ellerbe caught the ball just before it hit the ground. Ellerbe had filled in admirably for Ray Lewis when the linebacker had been out with an injury, and now, with the 17-year veteran leader back on the field, Ellerbe was making the athletic plays Ray could no longer make.

In two minutes the Ravens had twice denied the Patriots any points in the red zone. But Ed Reed continued roaming the sidelines during the entire fourth quarter telling anyone who would listen, "Not yet. Not yet. It ain't over yet."

Brady got the ball back with two minutes left, still trailing 28–13, and promptly drove to the Ravens' 22-yard line. He'd been hit repeatedly, rushed and hurried the entire game, and it had worn him down. The 13-year veteran had only lost two playoff games at home and never after leading at halftime.

Brady underthrew Brandon Lloyd, who had a step on Cary Williams in the end zone, and the Ravens cornerback came down with an interception. Brady had targeted Williams in the 31–30 Ravens win earlier in the season, and the corner was being tested again. This time it was Williams who closed out the Patriots' season.

"Keep the ball. Keep the ball," Reed shouted at Williams, instructing him to fall down in the end zone so the Ravens would have good field position on the 20 and not risk a fumble by running it out. He had mentored Williams for three seasons and referred to him as his "little brother."

As the clock wound down, John Harbaugh was looking for the cornerback who had just iced the game. Ravens videographers found him scouring the sidelines yelling, "Where is Cary Williams? Where is Cary Williams?" Harbaugh eventually found the player that Ozzie Newsome had signed off the Tennessee Titans' practice squad in 2009 in a scrum of teammates on the bench. He embraced him as a father would a son. "I am so proud of you," he said.

Three times the Patriots had driven deep into Ravens territory with nothing to show for it. The Ravens had stiffened and forced two interceptions and a fumble. It reminded me of the "rope-a-dope" tactic that Muhammad Ali used against George Foreman in "The Rumble in the Jungle" in Zaire in 1974. Ali had absorbed rounds of body blows against the ropes, protecting himself while Foreman expended all his energy. Then Ali knocked Foreman out.

Tom Brady and the Patriots offense had "punched themselves out" in driving up and down the field for the entire game. Then Bernard Pollard took the Ravens off the ropes with two devastating hits. Exhausted and hurt, the Patriots dropped passes and Brady made critical errors. New England piled up 400 yards of total offense but only one touchdown.

"You have the opportunity to win the game, and we came up short," said Tom Brady to *The Huffington Post*. "There's frustration in that we wish we could have done better. But they're not going to give it to you. We didn't earn it; they earned it. They played a good game."

Brady had thrown for 320 yards to Flacco's 240, but his two interceptions deep in Ravens territory cost him a chance at winning the game. The clock snafu at the end of the first half also loomed large. A touchdown there would have meant a two-score advantage for New England going into halftime. The Ravens had defended the short field brilliantly the entire game, allowing only one touchdown. "As the field got smaller, Ray [Lewis] and Ed [Reed] played a chess game with opposing QBs and, in many cases, they won," said Keith Mills of WBAL.

Ray Lewis finished with 11 tackles. "Ray Lewis brought that team together. He's a fighter. He has always been the Muhammad Ali of the NFL to me," said Bennie Thompson, former Ravens special teams player and coach. Lewis stormed the sidelines as the clock wound down. "They better be careful about my retirement party. It ain't started yet."

Joe Flacco high-fived a large contingent of Baltimore fans as he made his way to the locker room. The Ravens quarterback had engineered his first trip to a Super Bowl in his fifth season. He didn't pass for as many yards as Brady, but his throws had been impeccable, and his three second-half touchdown passes gave his defense a cushion that allowed them to be even more aggressive. His overall postseason performance was stunning to date—eight touchdown passes and no interceptions.

Ray Rice had plunged into the stands with Ravens fans, and CBS Baltimore's Jerry Coleman filmed it all. "We did it. We did it for Baltimore. We're going to the Super Bowl," Rice said. "Call American Express and cancel my trip to the Pro Bowl."

Kick returner and receiver Jacoby Jones, like Ed Reed, was going back to his hometown of New Orleans for the Super Bowl. Video on the Ravens Web site captured him in the locker room saying, "I'm going to the crib. The 504. Lord have mercy. Crawfish on me. God couldn't have blessed me with a better team."

When the game ended, John Harbaugh met his friend Bill Belichick at midfield and they shook hands. Jen Slothower of the NESN Sports Network reported that Harbaugh told the Patriots coach that the Ravens studied everything the Patriots did and had modeled their organization after them. Belichick congratulated Harbaugh on how well the Ravens played and shared how difficult it was to prepare for Baltimore.

It was a much more restrained and humble Harbaugh than the coach who had been yelling, "We're going to the Super Bowl! We're going to the Super Bowl!" a few minutes before. He had adjusted to the moment and understood its symbolic meaning. He and his Ravens had finally risen to the top of the AFC, and an acknowledgment from Belichick, the person who had made an unsolicited late-night call to Steve Bisciotti to endorse his candidacy for the Ravens job in 2008, was important to him. He was the Harbaugh brother who had worked his way up through the coaching ranks just as Belichick had done and he knew how to say thank you.

Then Belichick and Ed Reed had a brief conversation. The Hoodie told the veteran safety to "finish it." The last player to leave the field, Reed clutched a copy of the *Baltimore Sun* front page that read, "AFC Champions!" He was doubled over on the sidelines laughing hysterically as reporters stood over him, their microphones at the ready. He kept laughing as he got up and ran off the field waving the front page, never saying a word.

10. One Play

I see him in mud, in snow, in dust, helmet down,
face a shadow, dragging two, three, would-be tacklers
for five, ten yards a clip, or breaking into open field
with a switchblade flick of his shoulders
and cutting to the end zone. The game
lay dead at his feet.

—Alan Kaufman

FORTY-NINERS quarterback Colin Kaepernick awaited the snap in shotgun formation. It was first and goal on the Ravens' 7-yard line with less than three minutes remaining in Super Bowl XLVII. On the previous play, running back Frank "The Inconvenient Truth" Gore, as he was called by 49ers fans, had rumbled like a tractor-trailer down a mountainside interstate for 33 yards and stepped out of bounds at the Ravens' 7. The rookie quarterback had led a furious comeback to trail 34–29 after being down 28–6 early in the third quarter.

The Ravens' defensive line stood with their hands on their hips. They were gassed, breathing hard. From my seat on the second level at the opposite end of the stadium, they collectively appeared to be on the verge of toppling over. As they looked into the eyes of their 49ers opponents, they saw younger, faster, and stronger versions of themselves.

"Bend, don't break," yelled Danny Glazer from Pikesville, Maryland, who was sitting behind me. "Watch the sneak!" Glazer was wearing a Joe Flacco jersey with purple strands of Mardi Gras beads and a purple camouflage bandana. He had started following the Ravens at the age of 11 in 1996. "We're going to win this game," he said.

The entire season had come down to one last goal-line stand. For the Ravens it was the end of an era that had lasted for the team's entire existence—the Ray Lewis era—and number 52 was leading the defense one last time, with the outcome of Super Bowl XLVII hanging in the balance.

"My favorite part ever was the conversations we were having in the huddle on the goal line," said Lewis at the press conference after the game. "There was no panic."

Vernon Glenn, sports anchor for KRON in San Francisco, was standing on the 49ers' sideline. "I was thinking that we needed to get out of town fast. We had a parade to put on in the Bay Area on Tuesday afternoon. I had no doubt that the 49ers were going to win because that's the way we'd played all year."

Rookie Colin Kaepernick was starting his 10th game after replacing an injured Alex Smith. He had a strong arm and ran like a cheetah in long strides, covering 5 yards at time. While at the University of Nevada, the tattooed signal caller had been the only player in NCAA history to pass for more than 10,000 yards and rush for 4,000. But in the first half of the game the rookie had been erratic. He overthrew Randy Moss in the second quarter and Ed Reed swooped in for an interception. He had rushed throws, and the 49ers had been behind the entire game.

Forty-Niners coach Jim Harbaugh had made a risky decision when he named Kaepernick as the starter over Alex Smith in Week 13 against the Rams. Smith had gone 19–6 with one tie as the 49ers signal caller since 2011. He had suffered a concussion against the Rams in Week 10 of the 2012 season and never returned as the Niners quarterback. Harbaugh, a former NFL quarterback, had turned Alex Smith's lackluster career around in 2011, but now he benched him.

One of Smith's six losses had come during the 2011 season in Baltimore. The 49ers had a record of 9–1 when they arrived at

M&T Bank Stadium on Thanksgiving night to play the Ravens. Smith had launched a bomb for a 79-yard completion in the second quarter to Ted Ginn, Jr., who caught the ball over his shoulder. It was the most spectacular play I'd seen all season. Fortunately for the Ravens, it was called back for a penalty. The Ravens defense, ranked third in the NFL in 2011, sacked Smith nine times that night, and the Ravens won 16–6.

Now the 49ers started a more dangerous quarterback in Kaepernick, one who could run and pass and who had more natural ability. He reminded me of a cyborg—half human and half an unstoppable scoring machine. He destroyed defenses. Against the Packers in the divisional round game on January 12, he faked a handoff and ran 56 yards for a touchdown in a 45–31 victory.

Kaepernick's size and speed had worried me before I left Baltimore, and he was still on my mind as I walked through the French Quarter before the game with my college friend Wyck Knox, a 49ers fan. The 49ers rookie had a better team behind him than Robert Griffin III, whose Redskins had already beaten us. The Ravens defense could no longer dominate an offensive line as they had in 2011.

The 49ers, like the Ravens, had also endured a devastating loss in the 2011 AFC Championship. San Francisco punt returner Kyle Williams had fumbled a punt in overtime against the Giants, all but giving the G-men a field goal and a trip to the Super Bowl. The fans from both cities deserved a trip to the Crescent City.

The pregame crowds on Bourbon Street paraded in Ravens purple and black and 49ers red and gold. Purple beads rained from balconies. Spontaneous outbursts of each team's cheers reverberated through the French Quarter. San Francisco fans chanted the Harbaugh family cheer that had been authored by Jack, the father, when John and Jim were growing up.

"Who's got it better than us? Noooobody!" Ravens fans countered by bellowing their "Seven Nation Army" chant from the White Stripes song. The cacophony sounded like a deranged choir.

Ravens fans I spoke with claimed that by Thursday we had taken over Bourbon Street, with a steady stream of 49ers fans mixing in as the weekend progressed. The Niners had won all five of their previous Super Bowls—led by quarterbacks Joe Montana and Steve Young—and though their fans hadn't been in a Super Bowl since 1994, they seemed confident of a victory.

I had been to New Orleans to hear music at Jazz Fest and to attend weddings, Mardi Gras, and conventions of chemists, librarians, food technologists, and plastic surgeons—but never to watch a football game. This was an assemblage of football fans in a garden of earthly delights—crowds with Hurricanes and Blackened Voodoo beers milling about amid a raucous din of blues, zydeco, and Cajun rhythms.

I had two plates of jambalaya before the game and pondered the similar eccentricities of Baltimore and New Orleans. The delectable lump meat from the blue crab, *Callinectes sapidus*, can readily be found in the cuisine of both burgs. Both cities have vibrant ports lined with freighters and container ships headed to the Far East. Each had produced numerous literary figures, too. Baltimore had once been home to Edgar Allen Poe and F. Scott Fitzgerald. New Orleans claimed Walker Percy, Anne Rice, and John Kennedy Toole. William Faulkner had written his first novel there and had walked the streets trying to peddle his early manuscripts.

Both towns possessed unique charms as well as challenges. Drugs, crime, and poor schools plagued both cities. But the towns shared an overwhelming obsession with football. New Orleans had embraced the Ravens fans. "They love us," said Ravens fan Steve Sneckenberger of Harford County in Maryland. "Saints fans hate Goodell, but they hate the 49ers more."

There was no love for NFL Commissioner Roger Goodell in the Big Easy on Super Bowl Sunday. "New Orleans is grateful to host the Super Bowl but we got hosed by the commish on the bounty scandal," said Laurent LeBien of Metairie. The scandal had involved Saints defensive coordinator Gregg Williams, who had been paying bonuses to players for lethal hits on the other team's best players. The NFL had suspended Saints players and coaches, including Williams and head coach Sean Peyton, for the entire 2012 season. If the sanctions hadn't been so severe, according to LeBien, this might have been the year that the Saints would be playing the Ravens in the Superdome for a Lombardi Trophy. "The NFL ripped the guts out of the Saints for something that other teams were doing," said LeBien. "We received the harshest penalties ever waged against an NFL team. They suspended our head coach."

I saw dozens of Saints jerseys as we walked up Bourbon to Poydras toward the Superdome. A Dixieland band played from a skyscraper rooftop. It was sunny and 60 degrees in the Quarter and a short walk to the game.

We had accidentally fallen in with the 2:52 Ravens March in honor of Ray Lewis that had launched from Decatur Street eight minutes before 3:00 P.M. Baltimore sports personality Nestor Aparicio had organized the march, which was scheduled to travel 17 blocks, one block for every season Lewis played. The Ravens linebacker, however, hadn't had the best of weeks leading up to the Super Bowl. He had taken some off-the-field hits to his reputation and legacy.

USA Today ran a story on the families of the Atlanta stabbing victims who still believed after 13 years that Ray Lewis got off easy for his alleged cover-up of the events that took place in the Cobalt Lounge in the Buckhead neighborhood on January 28, 2000. Richard Lollar and Jacinth Baker had been murdered in a brawl that had involved members of Lewis's entourage. "I live with that every day," Lewis told the *New York Times* just after the Super Bowl. "You maybe can take a break from it. I don't. I live with it every day in my life."

Sports Illustrated had also broken a story that claimed that Lewis had used a deer antler spray that included a banned performance-enhancing substance called IGF-1 in an effort to heal his damaged triceps. Lewis denied the allegations, and the *Baltimore Sun* interviewed Dr. Roberto Salvatori, a professor of medicine at Johns Hopkins who specializes in endocrinology and metabolism. Dr. Salvatori said that even if Lewis did use the spray, his body would not have absorbed the banned substance in the process.

For two decades, Lewis had been one of the more complex figures in professional sports. He had been accused of murder and then celebrated for his efforts in the community. He had been called a thug and a spiritual leader. His football skills had deteriorated but he was still capable of defending the run better than most middle linebackers. He was revered in Baltimore but looked upon with skepticism—and worse—everywhere else.

All these attributes had made him the perfect match for Baltimore, a city with insurmountable problems and a reputation for gutting its way through them. As the face of the franchise, Ray Lewis had never made football look easy or pretty, and the city loved him for it.

"In Baltimore, you couldn't go anywhere without seeing a No. 52 jersey," wrote John Sears on the WNST Web site. "The grocery store, the bar, school; he was everywhere. He became the King of Baltimore. He represented us. He personified us. His intensity, his drive, his passion. We all bought in."

He symbolized the city's struggle to be more than an afterthought between Washington and New York. He had been a Raven for 17 years and approached every play with a ferocity that resonated with the city. No matter how damaged he was, Lewis had put in the sweat equity that earned him his union card as a Baltimorean.

As we arrived at our seats on the second level overlooking the Ravens end zone, 49ers fan Wyck Knox shared with me that "Ray Lewis is the fifth or sixth best linebacker in this game. Patrick Willis, Ahmad Brooks, Navorro Bowman, and Aldon Smith of the 49ers are all better than he is and Suggs as well." Perhaps, based solely on ability at this point in their careers, but only future seasons would show whether any of those players could rally a team from the edge of the abyss to the Super Bowl, as Lewis had done for the 2012 Ravens.

On the field, pregame festivities were under way. Brothers John and Jim Harbaugh exchanged a hug. Jim looked uncomfortable as his brother pulled him close, but John wasn't going to let a world championship get in the way of one of his main priorities: family. Jim admired him for that.

"I'm like half the coach he is," Jim Harbaugh told the *Baltimore Sun* about his brother. "He's got the ability, when he's around his wife and daughter, to make it all about them. Some coaches have to work around the clock, because they're just not as productive as John. But it comes back to ability. He just has a lot of ability."

Childs Walker and Mike Klingaman provided the most detailed portrait of the brothers' relationship in a *Sun* article published a few days before the game. According to these authors, the brothers Harbaugh were reluctant to make the Super Bowl about their relationship and wanted the public's attention focused on the players.

John, the older brother, was more laid-back than his overly competitive sibling. In their younger days, he had smoothed over card games with their friends when Jim had marked the deck. He had broken up fistfights with his brother and neighborhood kids over backyard football games.

"It's unbelievable. When we dreamed of playing in the Super Bowl in the backyard, we were playing in it, not coaching it," John told Brian Billick in a pregame interview for the Ravens' postseason DVD.

Jim had played quarterback for legendary coach Bo Schembechler at the University of Michigan, and his talent and reputation as a fierce competitor led him to the NFL as a Chicago Bear, Indianapolis Colt, San Diego Charger, and Baltimore Raven. He came within a dropped pass of taking the Colts to a Super Bowl in 1995.

Jim has a visible edge: he's aggressive and prickly and not shy about belittling reporters who ask ridiculous questions. "He will fight you for anything, whether it's a game of cards growing up or whatever, he was going to try to find a way to win no matter what," John Harbaugh told the *Baltimore Sun*. "I think that's what made him a great player. . . . It's what makes him the man he is. He is also really talented."

The smaller John had played defensive back at Miami of Ohio. He had worked his way up through the college assistant ranks to the coaching staff of the Philadelphia Eagles as special teams and defensive backs coach and then to Baltimore as head coach of the Ravens. "The Ravens didn't see [John] Harbaugh as a special teams coach. They saw him as someone who had the discipline, confidence and imagination to take them to the next level, and they were right," wrote CBSSports.com's Clark Judge.

His friends called him "Harbs" in that wholesome and nasally Midwestern accent because he was "a good guy." For the most part, John was the polar opposite of Jim—approachable and affable. It was evident in a childhood picture published on SI.com. John is smiling as he does today, and Jim is pensive. John had always been the coach. Even as a player he congratulated other players on tackles and good plays. "He can teach [the game] and he can teach it to everybody," said Jim in the *Sun* article. When it came to football style, the Harbaugh brothers agreed on the "grind some meat and rattle the molars" approach used by Schembechler at Michigan.

"That's straight Jerry Hanlon, Bo Schembechler, you know, Michigan, Big West, Big Ten football," John told NFL.com.

> That goes back to the roots. But, when Michigan would be ahead, I know Bo would be on the headphones with Jerry and say, "It's time to grind some meat." That would mean it's time to run the ball. It's four-minute offense, you know, they'd run that off-tackle play. And rattle the molars, you know, that's coming off the ball, that's trench warfare for football upfront. That's football.

Before every game in the regular season, their father, former college coach Jack Harbaugh, had sent each a FedEx package filled with analyses of the upcoming week's opponent, and for the Super Bowl his instructions on the Nola.com Web site to both his sons were simple: "Get ahead" and "Stay ahead."

Ravens photographer Phil Hoffmann remembered Harbaugh's first Ravens practice in Owings Mills before the 2008 season. Hoffmann was in the center of the huddle taking pictures of the new coach with his players. "You're killing me with all those clicks," Harbaugh had told him. Hoffmann realized that a former defensive backs coach wouldn't have had the experience of having his picture taken all the time. "He'd never been in that situation before," said Hoffmann. "I had to laugh during Super Bowl week thinking back to that practice. Now he had more than one hundred cameras clicking his picture at the same time."

I had never been to a football game in a domed stadium. The hallways of the Superdome were narrow and claustrophobic, and there was little room to maneuver. It was run-down and in need of a makeover. "This place is a dump compared to M&T Bank Stadium," said Danny Glazer. It had been built in 1975, and major damage to the roof incurred during Hurricane Katrina in 2005 had kept it closed for a year. More than $300 million was spent on renovations.

The bright fluorescent lights and reverberating din reminded me of playing the Madden football video game that my daughter, Mary Julia, had learned to play better than anyone else in our family. Before I left, we'd programmed the Ravens against the 49ers in the Superdome, and the computer-generated environment matched the artificially created one inside the dome.

It was a sterile place to watch football. Instructing the crowd were two in-game *Entertainment Tonight*–style hosts on the Jumbotron. They were cut from the same mold as television hosts Ryan Seacrest and Kelly Ripa. Before the game they reminded us when the game would start and when we would need to cheer. During the game they updated us on the score and other information such as, "Now the 49ers have the ball, and they are looking to even up the score." Duh.

As the clock approached game time, the tension inside the dome began to mount. Jennifer Hudson and a choir from Sandy Hook elementary school performed "America the Beautiful." I choked up thinking about those children and their parents. The voices of the choir echoed around the dome. Then Alicia Keyes performed "The Star-Spangled Banner." Her jazz piano improvisation of the familiar anthem provided a touching follow-up to the performance of the choir.

There's a moment near the end of the first verse—"Oh, say does that star-spangled banner yet wave"—when the Ravens fans who also follow the Orioles yell "O's!" on the "Oh." I had wished, just this once, that we could have restrained ourselves for this poignant moment at the beginning of the game. But the fans roared "O's" as loud as they could, and I mouthed it in silence.

The Ravens won the toss and deferred to the second half. They started the game on defense and forced a punt after Ray Lewis stopped 49ers running back Frank Gore on a third and 15.

Jacoby Jones returned the punt 17 yards to the Ravens' 49-yard line. Joe Flacco came out firing on the first series. He passed to Vonta Leach for eight yards and to Torrey Smith for 20 more in the right flat and moved the Ravens into scoring position. On a third and 4 from the 49ers' 13, Joe located Anquan Boldin on an inside seam route in the end zone. It was the same pass play used against the Patriots, and Boldin went up and caught it. The Ravens had stormed down the field to take a 7–0 lead.

Colin Kaepernick brought the 49ers back, mixing runs with Frank Gore and passes to Michael Crabtree and Vernon Davis to drive to the Ravens' 8-yard line. Davis had caught a 24-yard pass and was tackled by Ed Reed, who injured himself wrestling the gargantuan tight end to the turf. Then, with an amazing stride around the pass protection, Paul Kruger flattened Kaepernick for a 5-yard loss. The 49ers settled for a field goal and trailed 7–3.

Flacco now faced an onslaught of pressure from the 49ers defense. On one play he eluded two pass rushers to find Boldin for a 30-yard gain. But the drive fizzled in Niner territory when he was sacked by Ray McDonald, and the Ravens punted.

Kaepernick moved the ball down the field again to begin the second quarter. The 49ers were targeting Ray Lewis in the middle of the field, exploiting his weaknesses against the pass. They were forcing him to defend big, physical targets like Davis and Crabtree.

A big play allowed the Ravens to stop the drive, as they had done all year. On first down from the Ravens' 24, linebacker Courtney Upshaw hit 49ers running back LaMichael James and caused a fumble that the Ravens recovered. The rookie linebacker had missed James behind the line of scrimmage, but he didn't give up on the play, following it downfield and jarring the ball loose at the play's end.

Ravens tight end Ed Dickson made two pivotal receptions on the next drive—one for 23 yards that he caught as defensive back Donte Whitner arrived at the same time as the ball. Dickson turned his body away from Whitner to secure the catch. His catches set up a 1-yard touchdown pass to Dennis Pitta. The Ravens led 14–3 early in the second quarter.

Ed Reed intercepted Kaepernick on the next 49ers play from scrimmage. Kaepernick's ball sailed well beyond Randy Moss, and Reed was there to snare it.

Soon the Ravens faced a fourth and 9 from the San Francisco 14 and sent in the field goal team. But instead of kicking the ball, Justin Tucker took the snap and ran toward the right sideline for the first-down marker. He was thrown out of bounds 1 yard shy of the mark.

It was a gutsy play by the older Harbaugh brother. What happens if your kicker is injured on the play, in a Super Bowl? Who do you call on to kick the game-winning field goal? But John's expertise had been special teams before arriving in Baltimore in 2008, and he was going to use every aspect of the game—including one that he knew very well—to beat his brother. Special teams play could end up being the difference in a game of two evenly matched teams.

After stopping Tucker, the 49ers went three and out and punted the ball from the end zone. Jacoby Jones dropped the punt, recovered it, and then ran 11 yards to the Ravens' 44. Three plays later, Joe Flacco put Jones in the spotlight again. Joe took the snap from the shotgun, dropped back to pass, scooted up into the pocket, and threw a beautiful bomb on the run with a mere flick of his arm. Jacoby Jones had gotten beyond the defense and caught the ball as he fell backward untouched. He rose to his feet and sensed Dashon Goldson about to tackle him. So he headed right and spun around to avoid Goldson as he flew by him. Then he brought the play to a standstill as he confronted 49ers defensive back Chris Culliver. Jones shimmied and faked to the right as if he were Mick Jagger onstage. Culliver flinched, and then Jones turned the play into a footrace to the left side of the end zone. Neither Culliver nor Goldson was any match for Jones in the open field. The Ravens led 21–6 going into halftime.

The halftime show featured the singer Beyoncé and her former band Destiny's Child, which joined her for a few numbers. I had a side view of the singer on a heart-shaped stage. I listened to most of her show with my head in my hands, and though I recognized one of Beyoncé's songs, "Crazy in Love," from my daughter's playlist, I wanted the game to start again. No music could quell my anxiety. The Ravens had just played their best half of football of the season, but there were 30 minutes more to go.

Ray Lewis put his hands on Jacoby Jones's chest as the return man went to field the kickoff to open the second half. John Harbaugh had seen something on the tape that revealed a weakness in the return coverage for the 49ers. The highlights from NFL Films captured Harbaugh saying into the headset something about Jones "going right up the middle."

Jones caught the ball 8 yards deep in the end zone and made a slight turn to his right before racing 108 yards through a gap in the middle of the 49ers kick return coverage. It was the longest return for a touchdown in Super Bowl history. Jones had scored the last 14 points for the Ravens in spectacular fashion.

The 49ers and their fans were dazed. The Ravens led 28–6, and the 49ers offense was on the verge of giving the ball back to Baltimore, facing a third and 13. Wyck Knox couldn't believe his 49ers were being beaten this badly. He'd grown up in Georgia following the college Bulldogs and had been a 49ers fan since

"The Catch" in 1982 when Joe Montana found Dwight Clark in the back of the end zone, releasing the ball just before going out of bounds and ending Dallas's reign as America's team.

Knox had been to Atlanta with his mother, an Atlanta fan, the week before for the NFC Championship game to watch the 49ers beat the Falcons. "I don't like that tattooed quarterback," his mother had told him. Knox bought her a number 7 Kaepernick jersey anyway.

According to Knox, the 49ers had more talent on both sides of the ball—and they were stronger and faster. "But our defense can't stop the Ravens," he shook his head. "This should not be happening."

And then the lights went out in the Superdome.

It wasn't frightening—just distracting, like the halftime show. It seemed like a prank. My brother sent me a text from Kansas City. "What's going on?"

As the power failure continued, memories of Hurricane Katrina returned. I thought of the people who had lived for days in the Superdome without water. This was the city's first Super Bowl since that disaster. "The blackout was definitely a black eye," said resident Laurent LeBien. "We wanted to shine post-Katrina, and it was an embarrassment for the city." I thought of the New Orleans power company Entergy, which had left residents without power for two to nine weeks after the storm. "It was the ghost of Katrina," a friend texted. Seven years later, the memory of the storm had infiltrated the Super Bowl.

The 49ers were standing on their sidelines huddled around their coach. They were catching their breath and looking at all the time that remained. The Ravens were trying to do some cardio exercises to stay loose. They resembled an aerobics class. There were still 13 minutes left in the third quarter, but the blackout became its own period, and one that slowed down the black-winged birds from Baltimore.

When the lights came back on, the 49ers erupted. Within eight minutes, they'd trimmed the lead to 28–20. The comeback was highlighted by a 31-yard pass from Kaepernick to Michael Crabtree, who ran over the Ravens defense, breaking tackles before crashing into the end zone.

Joe Flacco and the offense went stale, going "three and out" on the next two drives, and the 49ers became the aggressor on both sides of the ball. The older Ravens seemed to have stiffened up during the blackout, and the Niners roared furiously back—overpowering them. On a Frank Grove 6-yard touchdown, Haloti Ngata's knees buckled and he was lost for the game.

Wyck Knox and the 49ers fans came back to life. They were on their feet, with everyone in the dome singing the Harbaugh family song. Joe Flacco passed a ball to Ray Rice, who had single coverage in the right flat. He was hit by Tarell Brown as he turned upfield and fumbled.

The 49ers had the ball again and were looking to score. Kaepernick had his eyes on the end zone, and he had Ted Ginn, Jr., open in the right corner. Cary Williams went high in the air with his arm extended to deflect the ball. The Niners kicked a field goal and cut the lead to 5 points, 28–23.

Joe Flacco had played a relaxed game all evening, and he didn't change course when the game was tight. He stayed cool and led his team down the field. It was a long drive that temporarily stalled the 49ers' onslaught. At the end of the third quarter, with the game on the line, he focused on the sure-handed receiver who had carried the Ravens throughout the postseason and who had been to the Super Bowl once before in a losing cause.

Anquan Boldin caught a short pass and rambled 30 yards into 49ers territory—dragging 49ers defenders with him. He caught another for 9 yards. The Ravens drove to the San Francisco 1-yard line but couldn't punch it in. Justin Tucker split the uprights, and the Ravens extended the lead to 8 points, 31–23. It was a critical drive that slowed the 49ers' momentum a little and gave the veteran defense time to catch its breath.

Still the rookie signal caller continued to steamroll the Ravens defense. He found Randy Moss for 32 yards. Then he ran the ball in from 15 yards out, taking long gangling strides, to cut the lead to 2 points, 31–29. The 49ers went for 2 points to tie, but the Ravens sent Ed Reed on a blitz and forced the rookie to throw toward the spot where Randy Moss was supposed to be. The ball sailed out of the end zone untouched. The Ravens defense had done just enough to disrupt the 49ers' blitzkrieg and preserve a slim lead.

With less than 10 minutes left, Joe Flacco faced a third and inches from his own 45-yard line. The 49ers' last four drives had produced three touchdowns and a field goal. By the end of the game, they would amass 468 yards. If he didn't get this first down, Flacco knew he would be playing from behind the next time he had the ball.

Joe assessed the Niners' formation when he came to the line and called out an audible that was captured by NFL Films. "Quick Charley left," Flacco yelled to the line and changed out of a Ray Rice run. He dropped back, pumped once, and threw a perfect 7-yard back-shoulder pass toward the right sideline for Boldin. Niners defensive back Carlos Rogers got his hand in there, but Boldin caught the ball and Rogers's arm as he crashed to the turf. "First down, Ravens!" Gerry Sandusky boomed to the radio audience.

Both players had wanted to catch the ball, but it was Boldin who "had to have it," to borrow a line from Jim Bouton's *Ball Four*. The play call was Unitas-like in its element of surprise, and it led to a field goal that provided some breathing room, 34–29.

John Harbaugh would say in the postgame press conference that Joe Flacco had "the guts of a burglar" on that third-down play. It kept the 49ers at bay for the moment and required that they score a touchdown rather than a field goal to take the lead. It was the last catch Boldin would make in the postseason and his final one as a Raven.

Starting with the Colts game in the wildcard round, he had made 22 catches for 380 yards and four touchdowns. The last 7 yards on the final catch prevented the 49ers from getting the ball back and led to a Ravens score. Joe Flacco would later call it the biggest play of the game.

Kaepernick rallied his troops for one last end zone invasion. With 3:25 left in Super Bowl XLVII, he passed up the middle to Crabtree on a crossing pattern, and the receiver gained 24 yards and nearly broke away from Corey Graham and Lewis just beyond midfield. On the next play, Frank Gore barreled 33 yards before stepping out of bounds at the Ravens' 7-yard line. The 49ers were going to score the go-ahead touchdown—it was just a question of when.

With first and goal from the 7, Kaepernick handed off to LaMichael James, who gained 2 yards. On second down from the 5, Kaepernick rolled to his right looking for Michael Crabtree in the right corner of the end zone. Crabtree had run a square out across the goal line.

The rookie quarterback had a brief window on the play to run the ball in, and his long strides probably would have reached the end zone in two steps. But he chose to pass. At the end of Crabtree's route, the receiver lightly pushed off on Corey Graham and turned around to catch the ball. Graham pushed him back from behind, and the poorly thrown ball, high and fast, zoomed past.

San Francisco tried the same play on third down, only Kaepernick released the ball earlier this time. Crabtree grabbed it at the 2-yard line, but as he turned to shoulder his way into the end zone, Ravens cornerback Jimmy Smith, assisting Corey Graham on the coverage, came up on his side and hammered him, sheering the ball out of the receiver's hands.

"[Smith] hit me in the face and I really couldn't see," Crabtree would later tell NFL.com. His vision was blurred until the next play. Smith, a 2010 draft pick who'd struggled to live up to expectations, had made his best defensive play of the season.

"One play," shouted a mic'd-up Ray Lewis to his defense. "One play and we win." It was the last down of his career as a Baltimore Raven.

The entire Superdome was on its feet. All my previous thoughts about winning the game had evaporated. I was trying to survive with my team. I could barely watch.

WBAL announcer and former Colt Stan White assessed the scene: "I was standing next to Anquan Boldin on the sidelines by the goal line. In the 2009 Super Bowl—Pittsburgh versus Arizona—the Steelers' Santonio Holmes had run by Anquan for the game-winning touchdown. I'm thinking, let them score so we have enough time to come back."

On fourth down, Colin Kaepernick tried Crabtree one more time. The 49ers must have believed that Michael Crabtree had a huge advantage over cornerback Jimmy Smith. As the ball snapped, Crabtree initiated contact with Smith at the line and they got tangled up for a few seconds.

Linebacker Dannell Ellerbe had busted through the line on a blitz. The Ravens had learned their lesson from the Redskins game when they didn't pressure rookie backup quarterback Kirk Cousins and he'd had plenty of time to find Pierre Garçon in the end zone. On this final goal-line stand, the Ravens blitzed Kaepernick on every play. The rookie was going to have to find a way to beat the Ravens while taking heat.

Seconds after the snap, Ellerbe was in Kaepernick's face. The linebacker knocked him backward, and the QB stumbled. Kaepernick rushed his throw toward the back of the end zone.

Crabtree had disentangled himself from Jimmy Smith by pushing him to the turf with his left arm. By the time he got free from Smith it was too late. When he reached up to catch it the ball was well over his head and past Crabtree.

"Did we just win the game?" I asked Danny Glazer. "Did we win?"

Forty-Niners coach Jim Harbaugh was apoplectic. He grabbed his right arm and emphatically pulled it down several times—making the sign of a holding penalty—in vain. He had wanted an interference call on Smith.

There had been contact, but it was initiated by Crabtree, not Smith. Crabtree took two steps off the line and extended his arms to block Smith's path and toss him to the side. He had been preoccupied with the cornerback, and his path to the end zone suffered from the delay.

Crabtree had saved his worst pass route for last of the three plays. The Ravens' pressure on Kaepernick reduced the time he had to deliver the ball, and Crabtree's first two tentative steps wasted valuable time. On what was specifically a timing play, Crabtree's delay was fatal.

From the end zone angle, Jimmy Smith clearly had his right arm around Crabtree before the receiver shucked him off. From my vantage point at the opposite end zone, the ball had been thrown high and was potentially uncatchable.

The referees had let both teams play a physical game. Smith's hold and release could have been considered incidental contact. The "no call" was the right call from the standpoint that the referees may not have wanted to alter the course of a game so dramatically.

Kaepernick's passes were thrown hard. He didn't try a fade or a touch pass. His ability to make these types of throws will determine his future as an NFL quarterback. It's an art Joe Flacco had mastered and used throughout the playoffs.

"I would have run Gore four times," said Wyck Knox seated next to me. The 49ers ran the same play three times in a row and denied Frank Gore and Colin Kaepernick the opportunity to get the ball in the end zone.

"I was pretty confident," said WBAL's Keith Mills about the goal-line stand. "Even if they scored a touchdown, I thought the offense would take it down and kick a field goal to win it. I had that much confidence in the offense. Now when it got to third down I really thought the defense would stop them. I think Colin Kaepernick really started to feel the pressure of the moment."

The Ravens defense had held again in a short field—something they had done all year. Mills believed that the Ravens red zone defense had covered up the weaknesses of Lewis and Bernard Pollard in the pass defense, because they didn't have as much territory to cover.

The game was still not over. The Ravens took over on downs backed up against their own end zone and ran the ball three times for 3 yards to the 8-yard line. Twelve seconds remained in regulation. "We should take the safety," I said to Danny Glazer. "It's too risky to punt the ball to Ginn, Jr. Two points don't matter." Glazer's friend John Lamb, who was sitting next to him, was listening to the radio call on a headset. "We're taking a safety," as soon as I mentioned it.

Ravens punter Sam Koch lined up for the kick. He took the snap and stood there as if he were getting ready to play keep-away. This time every player on the Ravens line blatantly committed a holding penalty. They tackled, grappled, wrapped up, tripped, and wrestled the 49ers down to keep them away from the punter. The infraction wasn't going to be called, and if the officials had blown their whistles the ball would have been placed half the distance to the goal and the Ravens would have punted again—running all the time off the clock.

Koch ran to his right, stopped, and waited for the 49ers to get through the road blocks on the line, and when they were a few yards away he ran right all the way out of the end zone. The strategy worked, and the punt team erased eight seconds off the clock, leaving only time for one more play.

Koch punted from the 20-yard line, and Ted Ginn, Jr., received the ball. Josh Bynes, the former practice squad player who had filled in for Lewis and Ellerbe during the Ravens' loss to Denver, tackled Ginn just past midfield, and the Ravens had won Super Bowl XLVII.

"San Francisco is midnight dreary right now, graveyard quiet," the poet Alan Kaufman texted me from Nob Hill.

Purple and gold confetti fell in the Superdome. The players and their families headed to the Lombardi Trophy presentation. Michael Phelps was near the stage. O. J. Brigance, the only player to win a Grey Cup and a Super Bowl for the city of Baltimore, was seated in his wheelchair next to the podium. Suffering from ALS, he was the first person mentioned by CBS announcer Jim Nance at the ceremony.

Brigance was a special teams player for the Ravens in 2000 when they won their first Super Bowl, and he'd made the first tackle in the game. He worked as the Ravens' senior adviser for player development and had been an inspiration to the team since being diagnosed with the disease in 2007. "The truth of the matter is, those men inspire me," said O. J. about the 2012 season. "They have helped give me a reason to get up out of bed every morning."

John Harbaugh took the podium and held up the Lombardi Trophy. "It's never pretty," he said, "But it is us." The Ravens coach had just won his first Super Bowl, and he couldn't enjoy it. He had shaken hands with his brother Jim and met Ravens owner Steve Bisciotti, who embraced him, but the look on John's face expressed concern. When he finally reached his dad, he asked how Jim was doing.

"I am totally devastated for my brother. It's strange—I don't really feel emotion right now," he told *Sports Illustrated.* "I never thought you could feel 100 percent elation and 100 percent devastation at the same time. But I learned tonight you can."

As a Baltimore Ravens fan, I understood Wyck Knox's pain. I couldn't celebrate with my friend, a 49ers fan sitting slumped over in the seat beside me. There had been moments of elation and moments of suffering in the game for both of us.

"It was quiet in the 49ers locker room. The voices were muddled," said KRON's Vernon Glenn. "No boom boxes. You could hear the other team down the hall celebrating. I still to this day don't know what they were doing calling the same play three times in a row."

Fans in Baltimore flooded the streets of Fell's Point, Canton, and South Baltimore to celebrate an incomprehensible season that was five years in the making. The 2012 Ravens began their climb to the Super Bowl in the spring of 2008 after they named John Harbaugh head coach and drafted Joe Flacco and Ray Rice.

"We never make it easy," Joe Flacco said. "It's the way the city of Baltimore is, and that's the way we are."

Flacco had been named Super Bowl MVP. He had played the game of his life. There were no longer any lingering doubts about his status as an elite quarterback in the NFL, especially since he had tied 49er Joe Montana for the most touchdown passes (11) in the postseason without an interception. He had come back from one of the most humiliating games of his career in the regular-season loss to the Broncos to quietly orchestrate one of the most electrifying postseason runs in NFL history.

Two months after the Super Bowl, Joe Flacco was asked to play Baltimore Colts legend Johnny Unitas in a bio-pic about number 19. He would portray Unitas in the football scenes from the 1958 NFL Championship. The film, *Unitas We Stand*, was written by Unitas's son Joe.

In New Orleans, in one of the most exciting Super Bowls ever played, Flacco wasn't acting the part of Unitas. He played as if he *were* Unitas. On the third-and-inches play in the fourth quarter, he had taken a page out of Unitas's playbook to fool the 49ers. It was similar to the Unitas slant to Berry in the 1958 game. "My dad would have liked [Flacco]," said Chad Unitas.

Flacco also shared a calm demeanor with Unitas. They were men of substance, not pretense. Unitas couldn't believe people wanted to buy his game jerseys. "That's my work shirt," he told his friend, Colts band leader John Ziemann. "I don't understand why they want it."

After signing a six-year $120.6 million contract in the weeks after the Super Bowl, Flacco drove to McDonald's for Chicken McNuggets. "Joe's the kind of guy who mows his own lawn," said John Eisenberg, a columnist for the Ravens. Flacco had lived with his family in the house he grew up in for the first three years of his NFL career—staring at a poster of his hero Tom Brady on the wall next to his bed.

Both Flacco and Unitas had brought championships to Baltimore in workman-like fashion. "John had a tremendous ability to concentrate," said former Colts tight end Jim Mutscheller. "He could sense things, feel things. [Flacco] has that same ability. He's played good football in big games. He's proven himself. You couldn't ask for more."

Ex-Colts defensive lineman Artie Donovan, another Hall of Famer from the glory days of the blue and white horseshoes, follows the Ravens closely. He put comparisons to Unitas into perspective. "I'm not a student of the arts or anything, but they sort of have the same personality. Joe maybe has a little more pizzazz," said Donovan. "After a touchdown pass, Johnny just walked off the field. Nobody was as good as John."

After the game I walked back down to the French Quarter with Wyck Knox. Bourbon Street throbbed like a giant purple parade dragon, and there was barely room to move. We escaped to Café du Monde for beignets and coffee. The wind off the Mississippi River was refreshing.

We walked down below the Quarter to Frenchman Street, where there are several good places to hear music. My favorite place was a hole in the wall called the Apple Barrel, so small it could barely hold 20 people. I'd been there in 2008 when the great swamp boogie guitarist Coco Robicheaux was still alive and he played his music until no one was left to listen. I thought about him, and I thought about the football fans in my family who'd also passed away. I thought about how much my Aunt Carita, Uncle Buddy, Queenie, Dino, and Carolyn Bartoli would have loved this Ravens team.

I thought about my father, who had watched the game with grade school friends on the Eastern Shore. I could see my mother in her Flacco jersey, the phones in her house outside Chicago turned off, screaming, "Come on Ray Lewis, one more time, you can do it!" I wished, too, my brother could have been at the game with me. We shared some of the same traits as the Harbaugh brothers. Brendan is the younger one, easygoing, the one everybody loved. As the firstborn, I was the brooding competitor.

Outside, an angry 49ers fan approached me. "The only reason your team won that game was because the referees gave it to you," he told me in a disgusted tone. "Watch the replay. It was pass interference."

There had been times when I would have engaged this guy and said the wrong thing on purpose just to make him angrier. But I also knew that if I had been in his position, I'd be pissed that my team lost. I was a husband, the father of two children, and a football fan, in that order. My team had just won a Super Bowl. It felt good to walk away.

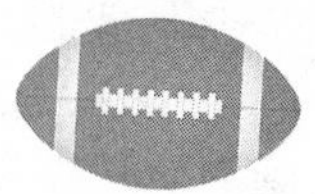

Acknowledgments

THIS BOOK would not have been possible without the support, friendship, and editorial acumen of Alex Holzman. I would also like to thank his staff of dedicated publishing professionals at Temple University Press, including Ann-Marie Anderson, Charles Ault, Sara Jo Cohen, Gary Kramer, and Irene Imperio Kull.

I am grateful for the assistance I received from writer Rafael Alvarez, who edited each chapter with the precision of a former city desk editor at the *Baltimore Sun*, and my researcher Phil Hearn, who collected a wide range of perspectives from each Ravens game. I am also grateful for the insight and wisdom provided by Stan Charles. We share an undying passion for Baltimore sports teams. I wish to express my thanks to photographers Phil Hoffmann, Sabina Moran, and William Hughes for providing stirring visual imagery of the season and to the late David Halberstam, Mark Kram, and John Steadman for their inspiration. Finally, I would like to thank John Ziemann for being there every step of the way.

Credits for Epigraphs and Photographs

Introduction: From "Wedding Photo, 1963," by Dean Bartoli Smith, originally published in Dean Smith, *American Boy* (Washington, DC: Washington Writers' Publishing House, 2000). Reprinted by permission of the author.

Chapter 1: From "The Consolation of Philosophy," by Jane Satterfield, originally published in Jane Satterfield, *Shepherdess with an Automatic* (Washington, DC: Washington Writers' Publishing House, 2000). Reprinted by permission of the author.

Chapter 2: From "Intercept," by Douglas Storm. Reprinted by permission of the author.

Chapters 3 and 9: From "Ars Ball Poetica," by Scott Hightower. Reprinted by permission of the author.

Chapter 5: From "Wanted," by Shirley J. Brewer. Reprinted by permission of the author.

Chapter 6: From "Opening Night," by Melody Compo. Reprinted by permission of the author.

Chapter 7: From "Elegy for Johnny Unitas," by Moira Eagan. Reprinted by permission of the author.

Chapter 10: From "Toby Parish," by Alan Kaufman. Reprinted by permission of the author.

All interior photographs courtesy of Phil Hoffmann.

Media Sources

105.7 The Fan, *The Monday Morning Quarterback*

BaltimoreRavens.com

Baltimore Sun

CBS Baltimore

CBS Cleveland

CBSSports.com

Dawg Pound Daily

ESPN

Fox Sports

Houston Chronicle

Huffington Post

KRON

NESN Sports Network

New York Post

New York Times

NFL Films

NFL Films: A Football Life: Cleveland 1995

NFL Films: Ray Lewis: A Football Life

NFL.com

Nola.com

Pittsburgh Post-Gazette

Press Box

ProFootball-Talk.com

Orioles Hangout (Ravens section)

Showtime, *Inside the NFL*

Sirius XM radio show host Adam Schein

Sports Illustrated, SI.com

The Byrne Identity blog

The Education of a Coach by David Halberstam

The Ravens' Postseason DVD: *NFL Super Bowl XLVII Champions: 2012 Baltimore Ravens*

Washington Post

TheNFLchick.com

USA Today

WFNY (Waiting for Next Year) blog

WBAL

WJZ-TV

WNST.net

Dean Bartoli Smith covers the Baltimore Ravens and the Orioles for *The Baltimore Brew.* His sportswriting has appeared in *Press Box, Fan Magazine, Baltimore City Paper,* and on the websites Patch.com and the Midnight Mind Review. He is the director of Project MUSE at Johns Hopkins University and the author of *American Boy,* a volume of poetry.